G. William Domhoff is a professor of psychology and sociology at the University of California, Santa Cruz. The noted author of *Who Rules America?* (Prentice-Hall/Spectrum Books, 1967), Mr. Domhoff has written numerous books and articles on the subject of political and social power.

Prentice-Hall International, Inc., *London*
Prentice-Hall of Australia Pty. Limited, *Sydney*
Prentice-Hall Canada Inc., *Toronto*
Prentice-Hall of India Private Limited, *New Delhi*
Prentice-Hall of Japan, Inc., *Tokyo*
Prentice-Hall of Southeast Asia Pte. Ltd., *Singapore*
Whitehall Books Limited, *Wellington, New Zealand*
Editora Prentice-Hall do Brasil Ltda., *Rio de Janeiro*

Quantitative Approaches to Political Intelligence: The CIA Experience

Other Titles of Interest

A Westview Special Study

Quantitative Approaches to Political Intelligence: The CIA Experience
edited by Richards J. Heuer, Jr.

Bridging the gap between the scientific approach to international relations and the intuitive analysis of the government foreign affairs specialist, this book reports on a concerted effort by the CIA to apply modern social science methods to problems confronted by political intelligence analysts. The unique experience gained through this CIA program holds lessons for both the scholar and the practitioner of international relations. The studies collected here demonstrate to the government analyst that systematic methods can be relevant to his needs, and show the social scientist that his skills can be applied to problems of direct interest to the foreign policy community. The book evolved from a panel presented at the Eighteenth Annual Convention of the International Studies Association in St. Louis in March 1977. The first chapter discusses the CIA's overall experience in applying quantitative methods of political analysis; seven subsequent chapters report on applications of specific methods as diverse as regression analysis, multidimensional scaling, Bayesian statistics, and cross-impact analysis.

Richards J. Heuer, Jr., is chief of the Methods and Forecasting Division of the CIA's Office of Regional and Political Analysis. He has had over twenty-seven years of experience with the CIA and received his M.A. in international relations from the University of Southern California.

Quantitative Approaches to Political Intelligence: The CIA Experience

edited by Richards J. Heuer, Jr.

Westview Press / Boulder, Colorado

A Westview Special Study

The views and conclusions contained in this book are those of the authors and do not necessarily represent the official policies, either express or implied, of the Central Intelligence Agency or the U.S. Government.

Published in 1978 in the United States of America by
    Westview Press, Inc.
    5500 Central Avenue
    Boulder, Colorado 80301
    Frederick A. Praeger, Publisher

Library of Congress Cataloging in Publication Data
Main entry unter title:
Quantitative approaches to political intelligence.
    (A Westview special study)
    1. United States. Central Intelligence Agency. 2. Intelligence service—United States. 3. Social science research. I. Heuer, Richards J.
JK468.I6Q36   327',12'0182   78-3781
ISBN 0-89158-096-4

Printed and bound in the United States of America

Contents

Preface

Scholars who emphasize the scientific approach to the study of international phenomena commonly despair of having their voices heard in the councils of government, while most government analysts are equally pessimistic that anything useful will come from what they regard as the pseudo-scientific endeavors favored by many academic political scientists. This book is intended for both scholars and government analysts of international relations, but especially for those who are concerned with bridging the gap between the two.

The common ground between scientist and government analyst has not been well developed. The studies collected together here are the fruits of a concerted effort by the Central Intelligence Agency to apply modern social science methods to problems of concern to political intelligence analysts. By bringing together a number of examples of our work under one cover, I hope to demonstrate to the government analyst that systematic methods can be relevant to his needs, and to encourage the scientist to apply his skills to problems of direct interest to the foreign policy community.

Chapter 1 discusses CIA's overall experience in applying quantitative methods of political analysis. The following seven chapters report on specific applications of various methods. Although several of the studies were written specifically for a nongovernment audience, all report on official work done for CIA. As is our habit, all authors have striven to avoid methodological jargon, writing so as to be understood by the informed layman with little or no quantitative training.

This volume grows out of a panel with the same title presented at the Eighteenth Annual Convention of the International Studies Association at St. Louis in March 1977. Four papers were presented to the academic community on that occasion as a sort of progress report on our efforts. Strong encouragement from our academic colleagues and the initiative of the publisher have now resulted in the revised and expanded work presented here.

It is not feasible to acknowledge by name all those who made this research possible, who contributed to it, or who helped to prepare the manuscript. Suffice it to say that it was a group effort, but that any deficiencies in what follows are obviously my own responsibility.

Richards J. Heuer, Jr.

Quantitative Approaches to Political Intelligence: The CIA Experience

1

Adapting Academic Methods and Models to Governmental Needs

Richards J. Heuer, Jr.

In response to a policy directive by CIA director William Colby to experiment with the application of what are, for CIA, unconventional methods of political analysis, small methodology staffs were established in the summer and fall of 1973 in the two CIA offices dealing primarily with political analysis. Although CIA has been innovative in the application of new methodologies in other fields, e.g., economic modeling of Soviet defense expenditures and information storage and retrieval, to name but two of many fields, the behavioral revolution in academic political science has been virtually ignored by the Agency and the intelligence community as a whole.

A reorganization in December 1976 combined the two methodology units and their parent offices into what is now the Methods and Forecasting Division of the Office of Re-

This is a revised version of a paper entitled "Adapting Academic Methods and Models to Government Needs: The CIA Experience" originally presented to the Eighteenth Annual Convention of the International Studies Association, St. Louis, March 16–20, 1977. The original paper was also presented at the Conference on Military Policy Evaluation: Quantitative Applications, held at the Strategic Studies Institute, U.S. Army War College, June 2-4, 1977. It appears in James A. Kuhlman, ed., *Studies in National Security*, vol. 3 (Leyden, Netherlands: Sijthoff International Publishing Co., 1978).

gional and Political Analysis (ORPA). The Methods and Forecasting Division is charged with studying analytical techniques employed by academia and industry, and then testing, adapting, and applying selected techniques to the needs of the political intelligence analyst. These are largely, but not exclusively, quantitative or computer-based procedures.

The product of the division's efforts is disseminated throughout the intelligence and foreign affairs community in the same manner as other intelligence reports. It is in this respect unique within the community, since other quantitative political research done for the State and Defense Departments, as well as for CIA, has normally been handled at the research and development level, i.e., contracted out, with the results often enjoying greater dissemination and acceptance outside of government than within it. Neither the State nor Defense Department has a methodology component integrated into the day-by-day political intelligence production process. Even at CIA we have made but a small beginning.

The following chapters present the results of some of our methodological work and show the kinds of techniques being employed. Other techniques we have used, but which are not discussed in this book, include elite analysis, election forecasting and simulation of election systems, gaming, Delphi, Nominal Group Technique, multiattribute utility analysis, and the operational code approach to the study of foreign leaders. This chapter attempts to synthesize our experience and some of the lessons learned in four years of trying to apply social science methods to political intelligence analysis. It seeks to answer the following questions: How and why do the Central Intelligence Agency's political research objectives condition its methodological procedures? What kinds of methods and techniques seem particularly well suited to the Agency's needs? And how successful have we been in gaining recognition of the role of quantitative methods within an organizational culture that is, and certainly must remain, by and large methodologically traditional in its political research?

The application of Bayesian statistics in estimating the probability of military attack was our first major project, initiated in response to a specific suggestion from Mr. Colby. The procedures developed for this purpose are described in chapter 2. The Bayesian analysis projects and those employing several other techniques were designed around a panel of experts, which meant gaining assistance from other analysts accustomed to traditional research procedures. Our early efforts benefited greatly from Mr. Colby's personal support, as the simple statement that the director liked our work opened many doors—and minds. The initial attitude of country analysts toward our unconventional proposals typically ranged from skepticism to hostility. Equally typical, however, has been their postproject appraisal that the work was interesting and well worth doing.

The original members of our office started by accepting the judgment of our critics that the Agency's approach to political analysis was antiquated, and that many useful techniques that had become routine in academia were being ignored by the intelligence community. Apart from the suggestion of Bayesian analysis, however, there was no guidance from above or consensus within the office on the specific directions which would be most fruitful. It was necessary, therefore, to take a broad look at the existing international relations data bases and theoretical models, as well as at specific analytical techniques. During the early part of that look, it became apparent that social scientists commonly define policy-relevant research far more broadly than the foreign policy community does, and that there were not a great many relevant methods and proven models ready-made for our use. We had to select from among many techniques those relevant to persistent problems of intelligence analysis. We then had to adapt these methods to the specific problem context and to the requirements of a governmental organization producing reports, often on deadlines, to be read by policymakers rather than by academics.

There are, of course, very many similarities between academic and governmental research. Both try to explain events, and to use a sound understanding of the past and present as a foundation for estimating the future. There are also significant differences. Some of these originate in different practical concerns, others reflect more fundamental differences in perspective.

While the academic researcher is relatively free to define a problem in his own terms, our research problems are generally defined by the requirements of U.S. foreign policy. The academic researcher chooses a topic for which data are available, whereas it is often new problems (or old problems defined in new ways) for which the policymaker requires intelligence analysis. For these kinds of problems there is usually a serious lack of good and current data. The quantitatively oriented scholar can easily limit his work to those variables that can be operationalized, but the government analyst seldom enjoys that luxury. The issues he deals with are generally characterized by a large number of variables in complex and poorly understood relationships. Further, the government analyst is far more concerned with matters of presentation. He is writing for an audience that, by and large, does not understand the procedures or tolerate the jargon of social science methodology, and he must keep his presentation brief if he wants it read by persons in authority.

There are also more fundamental differences in perspective. The intelligence analyst is almost invariably concerned with the explanation and prediction of what he perceives to be unique events, not with searching for general patterns in events. He must explain the October 1976 military coup in Thailand and what it portends for the future stability of that country, not the correlates of domestic violence in general. Theoretical propositions may, of course, contribute significantly to these explanations and estimates. The intelligence analyst uses explicit theory when he can, and it would certainly be helpful if more tested theoretical propositions at a level of specificity relevant to his concerns were available for his use, but he is generally not consciously concerned with trying to develop or prove theory. The country analyst views that as the task of academia, not government.

Since theory is the basis for all explanation and prediction, one might argue that the intelligence analyst is just as concerned with theory as the academician, the only difference being that the intelligence analyst normally does not make his theories explicit enough to be tested systematically and critiqued by others. This is, of course, true, but it glosses over very real differences in perspective between the researcher searching for patterns and the government analyst focusing on individual events. While these two perspectives are complementary in theory, they tend to be contradictory in practice and to require different skills and methods. The principal differences concern the generality or specificity of the variables being studied. The variables studied by the quantitative scholar are usually too general and highly aggregated to be of use to the intelligence analyst. Also, the kinds of variables and relationships studied by the intelligence analyst are, as O'Leary et al. discovered in their examination of State Department research, usually so specific and so complex that they are not amenable to analysis with the currently available techniques of quantitative social science.[1]

Methodologists sometimes argue that the intelligence analyst is unable to operationalize his variables and then employ scientific methods, only because he doesn't ask the right questions. If the analyst made his theory more explicit, they say, at least some of the variables could be operationalized. The analyst, on the other hand, sees the methodologist as wanting to use a laborious procedure to deal with only a small part of the problem rather than the key issues. He feels the methodologist is trying to change the question in order to suit it to the method, rather than fitting the method to the research problem. The country analyst generally has firm ideas about what questions he wants to answer, and what questions the policymaker or policy-support community wants answered. If the methodologist cannot assist in answering *those* questions, then he is perceived as having little to offer.

Because of its focus on the seemingly unique event, most political intelligence analysis takes a different approach to the problem of probabilities than most academic analysis. The analyst relies primarily on subjective probability estimates rather than statistical probabilities. Bayesian analysis (see chapter 2) and cross-impact analysis (see chapter 3) both use subjective probability estimates. Classical statistics require that the analyst disregard the uniqueness of the individual case in order to focus on the uniformities in the mass of cases. Our political analysts are generally reluctant to do this, as it forces them to ignore too much relevant information. The analyst's ideal is to know enough about the country for which he is responsible, enough about its leaders and its culture and problems, to be able to explain and evaluate events on the basis of the unique factors operative at that particular time. He tends to be skeptical of any form of simplification inherent in the application of probabilistic models.

There are, of course, problems for which some of the variables can be operationalized, with explicit hypotheses being formulated and then tested through statistical analysis of empirical data. In chapter 4, regression analysis is used to test the relationship between economic conditions and Left voting in France, and chapter 7 describes a data base that can be used to test hypotheses concerning transnational terrorism. It is satisfying to work with this hard data, but there are all too few problems of current intelligence interest for which this kind of data is available. There is doubtless much more that could be done if time were available and country analysts were trained to think in these terms. Even under the best of circumstances, however, the application of classical statistics in political research would be far less common in our work than in academia.

As already suggested, our work differs from academic research in the most common source of our data. For quantification we have relied heavily upon expert-generated data, rather than upon events data, survey data, or aggregate data on national attributes. Many of our projects involve a panel of experts who are asked to make quantitative judgments— that is, to assign probabilities, values or ranks to items of information. CIA's greatest resource is its cadre of substantive analysts with first-class academic training who then come to the Agency and immerse themselves in a given specialty under circumstances which provide access to the full intelligence collection resources of the U.S. government. Our task is not to try to replace the subjective wisdom of these specialists with so-called objective data, but to use rigorous methodological procedures to explicate and exploit more fully the insights and judgment of these analysts. In chapter 5, for example, expert judgment is used to assign values to the variables in a model of political violence, and chapter 6 describes a content analysis project in which expert judgment provides the criterion for assessing which of a number of potential quantitative indicators provides the best measure of support for Brezhnev.

Because of these many differences between our work and that of the academic researcher, our present tendency is to draw somewhat less inspiration from the quantitative research in political science and international relations, and somewhat more from the techniques of futures research and management science.

Because this book focuses exclusively on methodologically oriented research, the reader might get the impression that this comprises a major portion of the Agency's analytical effort. It doesn't. It is only a very small part of the total political research effort, and it is bound to remain a small part. As long as intelligence research is directed toward answering complex questions such as what will happen in Yugoslavia after Tito's death, or what would be the consequences of Communist party participation in the Italian government, the narrative essay will remain the dominant form for intelligence estimates.

There is, however, an important role for rigorous procedures even in such complex estimative problems. Our work to date indicates that the kinds of analytical techniques which seem most useful for our purposes are those that help to trace the logical consequences of subjective judgments, extend the mental capacity of the individual analyst, force the analyst to make his assumptions explicit, or help to organize complexity. Group process techniques that structure interaction within a group of analysts working on a common problem are useful. Probabilistic explanations grounded in classical statistical procedures are also useful, but they are much less fundamental to our work than to academic research dealing with empirical theory.

We frequently ask ourselves how successful our efforts to introduce more systematic methods of analysis have been. One conservative measure of success of any bureaucratic innovation is simple survival. Having recently survived a major reorganization, there is reason to feel we have been successful enough to at least guarantee our continued existence as an Agency entity responsible for furthering methodological innovation in political research. This certainly represents progress when compared with our tentative beginnings in 1973. The distribution of our reports in many copies throughout the intelligence and foreign policy community serves as a periodic reminder to all recipients, including our own analysts, that the Agency's leadership is committed to experimenting with nontraditional techniques of political analysis.

The true test of success is not, however, the reports we produce ourselves, but the extent to which we serve as a catalyst in changing the attitudes and procedures of other analysts. Success comes when analysts in country or other functional divisions take the initiative in requesting our support, or themselves employ the techniques demonstrated in our pilot projects. In this respect, our success has been more modest than we might hope, but nonetheless sufficient to strongly encourage further pursuit of our goals.

In summary, the above review of our experience in applying methodological approaches to political intelligence analysis makes three principal points. First, CIA is well aware that different and more systematic approaches, such as those commonly associated with the behavioral revolution, have transformed much of academic international relations research during the past twenty years or so. Secondly, the different goals of this approach—its emphasis on empirical theory and on the kinds of problems that can be quantified—place rather severe and intractable limits on its applicability to the needs of government agencies concerned with foreign affairs, since most of the variables of interest simply cannot be quantified. Finally, despite these limitations, there is a role for more rigorous analysis in the Agency's political research, and there is an ongoing, active effort to define and to fulfill that role.

Note

1. O'Leary et al. conducted an empirical analysis of the types of variables and relationships analyzed by the State Department's Bureau of Intelligence Research (INR). The authors concluded that "analyses found in INR documents tend to be of the most demanding kinds, involving multivariate analyses with many discrete variables, in which the relationships are frequently nonlinear and involve important time lags. As a matter of fact, the kinds of relationships found in the great majority of INR analyses represent such complexity that no single quantitative work in the social sciences could even begin to test their validity." Michael K. O'Leary, William D. Coplin, Howard B. Shapiro, and Dale Dean, "The Quest for Relevance: Quantitative International Relations Research and Government Foreign Affairs Analysis," *International Studies Quarterly* 18 (June 1974): 228.

2

Bayesian Analysis: Estimating the Probability of Middle East Conflict

Nicholas Schweitzer

As adapted for use in political intelligence estimates, Bayesian analysis is a method of extracting more information than usual from evidence, and of encouraging analysts to consider alternative explanations of that evidence, through a formal procedure of probability assessments.

The purpose of the analysis described here was a continuing periodic assessment of events and the prediction of possible hostilities in the Middle East. The result was a well-received series of reports issued on a periodic basis over a two-year period. Unfortunately for our purposes here, the reports themselves are classified to protect the sources of information cited in them. The techniques employed in the reports are common knowledge, however. The core was Bayesian inference, but equal credit for the project's success must go to an adaptation of the Delphi technique.

Bayesian Analysis

The statistical formula which forms the basis for our analysis bears the name of the Reverend Thomas Bayes, who

This is an abridged version of a paper presented at the Seventeenth Annual Convention of the International Studies Association, held in Toronto, February 1976.

was the first to express this particular mode of inductive inference in precise quantitative form. His work, entitled "An Essay towards Solving a Problem in the Doctrine of Chances," was read posthumously in 1763 before the Royal Society, of which he was a fellow. The most accessible copy of it appears in *Biometrika* (December 1958, pp. 293-315). The formula is a tool of statistical inference, used to deduce the probabilities of various hypothetical causes from the observation of a real event. It also provides a convenient method for recalculating those probabilities in the light of a continuing flow of new events. Reduced to its simplest form —and it is by no means a difficult formula to begin with—the "rule of Bayes" states that the probability of an underlying cause (hypothesis) equals its previous probability multiplied by the probability that the observed event was caused by that hypothesis. Once the probabilities are assigned, which is the difficult part, the mathematics are as simple as $A = B \times C$. (A more detailed explanation of the mathematics involved is given in Appendix 1.)

One of the classic uses of this type of induction is described by Frederick Mosteller and David Wallace in "Inference in an Authorship Problem" (*Journal of the American Statistical Association,* June 1963, pp. 275-309). This was an investigation to resolve the disputed authorship of twelve of the Federalist papers, based upon the frequency per thousand words of various noncontextual words such as "upon," "also," "though," "although," "while" and "whilst." The rule of Bayes was used to derive the probability of Hamiltonian or Madisonian authorship for the papers, based upon observed frequencies of the telltale words in *The Federalist* and in other examples of their writing. The results, which are considered a classic example of the overwhelmingly strong inference that can attend this type of analysis, were in consonance with most contemporary assessments, assigning all of the disputed papers to Madison.

In the field of intelligence, a nearly perfect application for Bayesian inference has been developed to identify military units and installations which are seen in aerial photography. For example, groups of weapons, buildings, and local improvements may be observed, and the type of military unit—such as an infantry regiment or a motorized rifle battalion—may be immediately obvious. Often, however, certain typical features may be absent, or certain extraneous pieces of equipment may confuse the identification. In such cases, the inferential strength of the rule of Bayes has frequently been able to cut through the "noise" of a few contradictory items to assign a high probability to a particular type of unit.

An explanation of how this is done will serve as a useful introduction to the use of Bayes for political analysis. The starting point, the data base from which inference is drawn, is a set of probabilities for seeing certain identifying features in different units. For example, whereas a group of ten tanks may be a common sight in a motorized rifle battalion, ten tanks may very rarely be seen in an infantry regiment. Thus the following probabilities might be assigned: 0.90 or 90 percent that such a group of tanks would be seen if the unit is a motorized rifle battalion, and 0.10 or 10 percent that the tanks would be seen if the unit is in fact an infantry battalion. These probabilities, called the "objective probabilities," can be derived either from historical observation or from expert opinion. The early application of this technique drew upon the knowledgeable guesses of analysts in this field. These probabilities were later supplemented by a study of known units. When the probabilities associated with a whole range of identifying features and equipment are aggregated using Bayesian analysis, the type of unit under study often emerges clearly from the "noise."

This paper describes the application of Bayes to political analysis, an even more complex field in which there are no objective probabilities of events, and in which the historical examples of previous conduct are ambiguous or inapplicable. The political, economic, strategic, and social events of the world are imperfectly understood and difficult to measure. For example, what is the difference in significance between Shimon Peres saying "the Israeli military movements are strictly precautionary" rather than "the Israeli military movements are strictly defensive"? Which is more probable if Israel is seriously considering a preemptive attack? How much more probable? Would we be able to derive some form of objective probability from a catalog of previous use of those phrases and previous attacks? And how probable are such statements even if no attack is in the wind? The interpretation of public statements and troop movements is difficult, to be sure, but it is still our job to interpret them. Hence, to use a technique like Bayes it is necessary to turn to expert judgments expressed quantitatively. The values assigned are educated guesses and are imprecise, but they provide a starting point and at least a rough basis for comparison and analysis. Our experience suggests that it is relatively easy to induce analysts accustomed to qualitative expressions of probability to shift to numerical assessments. If we can face the challenge of assigning probabilities to such events, Bayesian analysis can allow us to squeeze a little more information from the data we *do* receive. One danger, however, is the ever-present tendency to attribute more precision to a number than is warranted, and it must continually be stressed that the numbers are only approximate.

It is only proper at this point to mention that individuals in the Agency have investigated the utility of this technique for many years, and that much of the acceptance of our current efforts is due to earlier experiments applying Bayes to the analysis of historical intelligence situations. As Mark Twain said, "Habit is habit, and not to be flung out of the window by any man, but coaxed downstairs a step at a time."

Delphi

The Delphi technique was developed by the RAND Corporation in the late 1940s as a systematic approach to soliciting, improving, and combining expert opinions on a subject. Its major points are:

- formulation of the problem under investigation in quantitative terms;
- interrogation of experts through questionnaire or interview;
- controlled iteration, in which the results are usually presented statistically and the anonymity of individuals is preserved.

Delphi has been used in hundreds of studies by government, business, contract research and development organizations like RAND, and academic institutions, often as a method of forecasting scientific and technological progress. It tends to break down barriers between disciplines and to stimulate creative thought through cross-fertilization from related and unrelated technical fields. It also tends to elicit ideas from experts in a setting that provides some of the benefits of large groups without the difficulties of group dynamics and personal competition. As will become apparent in the next section, these major components of Delphi were all incorporated in the Bayesian analyses.

A historical footnote at this point may lend credence to the premise that mere expert opinion can be used to investigate the labyrinthine corridors of international affairs. A study by Frank Klingberg in 1937 analyzed responses from 220 persons who were judged to be knowledgeable about world affairs. They were asked to rate from 0 to 100 the probability of war within ten years for 88 pairs of states. The results, as reported by Quincy Wright in *A Study of War* (pp. 338-340 in the abridged version) correlated highly with the orientation and sequence of entry of states into World War II. Wright's critique of the study was that "predictive results of some value for a few years ahead can be obtained from an analysis of expert opinions."

Specific Adaptation of the Techniques

There has been much adaptation in creating a workable vehicle for intelligence analysis. We have faced the realities of working with individuals who often are under time pressure, and have tried to develop a genuinely useful procedure without being Procrustean. There is often a conflict between pure theory and applied engineering. Although we do our best to satisfy both, we tend to favor the engineer.

The actual procedure for the reports is a periodic routine. On the first day of the period, each of a number of participating analysts submits the items of evidence he or she has seen since the last round which relate in any way to possible hostilities in the Middle East. The submission is in the form of one or two sentences summarizing the item, along with the date, source, and the classification. For example:

> The Egyptian war minister visited naval forces in Alexandria on 11 February. He asked officers and other members of the naval forces to continue their vigilance and to prepare to face any sudden military situation. (Cairo Radio, 12 February 1976, unclassified)

The choice of data is left entirely to the analyst, who is instructed to include anything he considers relevant and to exclude what can be judged to be irrelevant. Later the same day, a coordinator consolidates the items, resolving differences of wording, emphasis, and meaning, and returns the complete list of items to all participants. The analysts, working individually, evaluate the items and return the numerical assessments the following day. This information is then collated and disseminated as an intelligence report.

One of the central features of our studies is the use of a group of analysts rather than a single expert. This, more than anything else, influences the data-gathering process, the format of the publication, and the actual production procedure. The reasons for this approach are:

- to bring to the exercise a range of expertise beyond the experience of any single analyst or single Agency office, i.e., Arabists and Israeli specialists, and analysts specializing in political, economic, and military affairs are all represented;
- to supply a richer mix of evidence on the questions by asking each analyst to contribute anything he or she considers important. As most political, military, or strategic intelligence problems are reflected in a host of areas, such varied inputs as propaganda analysis, photographic interpretation, and logistic calculations are useful;
- to provide a balance of expertise in which the effects of organizational and individual bias are minimized.

It is an accepted fact that analysts in different offices will tend to place greater reliance on different types and sources of intelligence. The consolidated list of intelligence items, which is circulated to all participants without identifying the

contributors, provides an opportunity for each analyst to call
an item to the attention of his colleagues in other offices. To
avoid time-consuming group meetings, the problems of
scheduling, and group dynamics effects, each analyst works
on the probabilistic assessments individually and relays them
to the coordinator.

Another feature of the studies is that each periodic report
actually contains the intelligence items identified and used by
the participants, with only a paragraph or two of composed
text on the principal trends during the period. No attempt is
made to formulate or coordinate a lengthy textual analysis of
the situation. This allows the reader of the reports:

- to see the basic evidence rather than just a summary,
  and hence to understand better the analysts' assessments;
- to make his own direct assessments if he so desires, or
  just to keep up with the topic by viewing the evidence
  regularly;
- to maintain a concise chronology of the situation.

The ability to portray the results of the analysis graphically was one of the strongest arguments for using a quantitative method like Bayes, and the graphs in the publication
have been well received. The probabilities of the various
types of hostilities (the hypothesized events) are immediately
visible on a broken-line chart. This conveys much information at a glance, and seems to represent an advance in com-
munication over traditional methods of reporting, especially
in illustrating trends far more concisely and vividly than
do words. In addition, the range of estimates around the
central measure shows clearly and concisely how much disagreement there is. It is just possible that much of the success
of the reports is due more to this informative brevity than to

the validity of the estimative technique.

Another interesting procedure, also presentational, is the listing of all participants by name and office. This visibility is pleasing to the analysts, who normally endure considerable anonymity in their work. We do not identify analysts with their own individual trend line, however, because we found this promoted a slight tendency to want to manipulate the results if an analyst feels uneasy with the direction his assessment is taking. (The Bayesian procedure normally pushes the analyst faster and farther from his starting point than he would move if he were employing traditional intuitive procedures for revising judgments.) In order to obviate some of these problems, we have found it useful to develop a supplementary graphic which does allow participants to be visibly identified with an individual line. This graphic reflects the analysts' hunch opinions on a separate but related question. Although this chart is rather primitive methodologically, it too performs well as a barometer of change; once each individual chooses his position on the chart—as a hawk, a dove, or a middle-of-the-roader—the ups and downs are fairly consistent across the board. The trends are clear from month to month, and there is no need for all participants to agree on a single number.

Over the past few years, we have applied these techniques to the study of various situations involving a potential for hostilities, including the likelihood of a major North Vietnamese offensive during the dry season of 1974 (the year before the debacle), the prospect of Sino-Soviet hostilities from summer 1974 to the present, and the likelihood of Arab-Israeli hostilities from autumn 1974 to summer 1976. In the course of our projects, we have recognized many limitations and have harbored certain reservations about the applicability of the method; such limitations and reservations are discussed in Appendix 2. In many ways, the Middle East has been the most complex of our Bayesian analyses, has presented us with the greatest challenges, and has pushed us closest to the limits of the design.

A Middle East Example

The following description will catalog the questions which were investigated, and illustrate how the probabilities are calculated. Although the project was also carefully tailored to meet the needs of the participating offices and individuals, those matters are beyond the scope of this paper.

After much discussion of what questions would be relevant, approachable, and of interest to our government audience, four scenarios or hypotheses were set out:

- No major hostilities are planned by Syria, Egypt, or Israel within thirty days;
- Syria, either alone or in concert with other Arab states, plans to initiate major military action against Israel within thirty days;
- Egypt, either alone or in concert with other Arab states, plans to initiate major military action against Israel within thirty days;
- Israel plans to launch an attack against one or more Arab states within thirty days.

These four may not be mutually exclusive, but we have treated them as such for the purpose of calculating probabilities. We also know that we have not exhausted all the possibilities. Foreign policy analysts are all too familiar with the words of the elder von Moltke: "Gentlemen, I notice that there are always three courses open to the enemy, and that he usually takes the fourth."

At the inception of the exercise, each participating

analyst assigned a set of probabilities to these four hypotheses, based upon his understanding of the situation up to that time. These were the best starting estimates available. The sum of the probabilities had to equal 1, or 100 percent; that is, it was assumed that one of the four had to occur within thirty days. Generally, the hypothesis of no hostilities within thirty days was assigned a probability of from 0.7 to 0.95.

Subsequently, these estimates were changed, by assessing the evidence—from open and classified sources—in terms of each of the hypotheses and calculating the new probabilities according to the rule of Bayes. There is an independent set of figures maintained for each analyst, which is charted over time to show changes and trends.

For example, let us simplify the calculations by assuming only two hypotheses, that Israel is planning to launch a major offensive against Syria within thirty days, and that it is not, and further assume that an analyst has assigned the following probabilities to these hypotheses:

- Probability that Israel is planning to launch a major offensive against Syria in thirty days—10 percent or 0.1
- Probability that Israel is not planning such an offensive —90 percent or 0.9

Also assume that the following item arrives and that the analyst assigned probabilities to such a report surfacing, first assuming that Israel is planning an attack, and secondly assuming that it is not;

Israeli Finance Minsiter Rabinowitz stated that the nation's economic situation is one of war and scarcity, not one of · peace and prosperity. (Jerusalem Radio, 20 February, unclassified)

- Probability that this would be said if Israel is planning to launch a major offensive against Syria within thirty days—99 percent or 0.99
- Probability that this would be said if Israel is not planning such an offensive—90 percent or 0.90

By following the Bayesian formula, this information can be used to revise the probability that each hypothesis is true. The formula itself and the complete calculations are given in Appendix 1.

- Revised probability that Israel is planning to launch a major offensive against Syria within thirty days—0.12
- Revised probability that Israel is not planning such an offensive—0.88

Notice that the two prior probabilities added up to 1, or 100 percent, and that the revised figures also equal 1, even though the conditional event probabilities do not.

As this is a recursive process, in which a succession of events are assessed, the revised probabilities become the prior probabilities for calculating the effect of the next item, and the final set of probabilities for a period becomes the starting point for the next period's assessment.

Conclusions

Utility as a Predictor of Events

Upon completion, the Bayesian method results in an archive of evidence, evaluations, and predictions that lend themselves to various forms of evaluation. The main criterion for evaluation is the accuracy of prediction, although this may not be as straightforward as it seems. Because of the myriad variables in the prediction equation, an event may occur that was only 10 percent probable the day before, or an event that was scheduled to occur may fail to materialize. Thus, there have been times of great uncertainty during our reporting periods when the probability of certain hostilities rose, only to fall back again later. Does this mean that the high probability of the event was somehow in error? Rather, it would seem to mean that at the time the event could very well have occurred if other factors had coincided. The evaluation cannot really be considered "wrong."

Generally, our studies have successfully predicted non-events. That is, they showed that the evidence did not support any of the positive hypotheses of hostilities, and none of them in fact occurred during the period studied. In such a case, the point to be noted is how early the evaluations moved away from an indeterminate figure toward a strong probability of no hostilities. It has been our experience that the Bayesian calculations show this movement earlier than the analyst's intuitive judgment would. Until one of the positive hypotheses actually occurs during the course of a Bayesian exercise, it is difficult to know the predictive value of the technique. If such a positive event does take place, it would be possible to conduct a much more searching evaluation. What were the earliest indicators? What evidence was missing, overlooked or misperceived? When did the trend lines signal a significant alteration in the situation? How did the Bayesian assessment compare with other intelligence assessments?

Other Benefits to Participants and Readers

There is no magic and no inherent wisdom in Bayes. In simplest terms, the Bayesian technique consists of a statistical formula and a procedure for its use. It is an organizing device that allows an analyst to use his expert understanding of a situation to assess the likelihood of various hypotheses about an intelligence problem, and to evaluate fragments of evidence in terms of those hypotheses. The Bayesian formula then aggregates those numbers mathematically, rather than by the nonrigorous logic of human induction, into an overall set of probabilities. This has the following advantages.

(1) More information can be extracted from the available data because the technique allows each piece of evidence, central or marginal, to add its weight to the final assessment in a systematic way. Thus, a number of small items can outweigh a large one, and the probabilities are not at the mercy of the most recent or most visible item.

(2) The formal procedure has been shown to be less conservative than analysts' informal opinions, and to drive the probabilities away from fifty-fifty faster and farther than the analysts' overall subjective judgments do. This is often initially unsettling for the analysts, but most have admitted that they later agreed with the assessment.

(3) The procedure provides a reproducible sequence of steps for arriving at the final figures. A disagreement among analysts can thus often be seen as a disagreement over the meaning of certain items rather than an unresolvable difference of opinion.

(4) The formulation of the questions forces the analyst to consider alternative explanations of the evidence he sees, thus loosening the bonds of established opinions. In other words, he is asked to look at how well the evidence explains hypotheses other than the one he has already decided is most likely.

(5) The use of quantified judgments allows the results of the analysis to be displayed on a numerical scale, rather than through the use of such terms as "probable," "likely," "unlikely," or that gem "possible." In addition, the work of more than one analyst can be portrayed in graphic form, with ranges and averages.

(6) The mere fact that a team of experts is asked to assess periodically the evidence on an important intelligence question provides managers of intelligence production with a degree of assurance that the question is indeed being monitored effectively.

Applicability of the Technique

The starting point for any investigation, whether in intelligence or in an academic setting, must always be the careful formulation of the relevant questions. The Bayesian technique has definite limitations, and it can only be applied where certain criteria are met:

(1) The question must lend itself to formulation in mutually exclusive categories, such as war versus no war, or the development of a nuclear capability versus no nuclear development. If various overlapping possibilities enter into the picture, such as limited border harassment or the development of a purely peaceful nuclear capability, the results of any Bayesian formulation may be suspect.

(2) The question must be expressed as a specific set of hypothetical outcomes. The Bayesian approach would be useless as a predictor of "the pattern of future Middle Eastern relations." The question would at least have to be recast in terms of specific alternatives, that is, a set of scenarios of Middle Eastern developments. In this process, however, there would be a danger that the question would be so simplified as to render any answer irrelevant and uninteresting.

(3) There should be a fairly rich flow of data which is at least peripherally related to the question. For the question of nuclear development, for example, data on all related materials and processes would be relevant. If information is sparse, the technique is very sensitive to each item and may be less reliable.

(4) The question must revolve around the type of activity that produces preliminary signs and is not largely a chance or random event. For example, it would be fruitless to attempt to predict which military leaders will be in Cairo on a particular day. Bayesian analysis reacts only to preparations for and indicators of the hypothesized outcomes.

The Future of Such Analysis

We have found this technique to be a useful adjunct to traditional analysis. It is the frequently voiced opinion of various readers of the Bayesian reports that they are thought-provoking and represent an advance in communications over traditional methods. There is nevertheless a healthy respect and a continued need for the traditional analysis of complex problems that are beyond the limited scope of Bayes. Most of the research and writing in our office, the rest of the Agency, and the rest of the intelligence community will continue in the traditional mode, but we shall supplement it when appropriate with Bayesian analysis and other "new" methods.

Appendix 1:
The Statistical Basis for the Technique

The rule of Bayes is a statistical identity, derivable from the laws of intersection of sets and the definitions of conditional probability and mutually exclusive events. Most statistics textbooks contain the derivation, one source being Miller and Freund, *Probability and Statistics for Engineers*, pp. 29-32.

In symbols, the rule is

$$P(H_i|E) = \frac{P(H_i) \times P(E|H_i)}{\sum_{i=1}^{n} [P(H_i) \times P(E|H_i)]}$$

where E is an event, an "item" of intelligence;

H is an hypothesis, an hypothesized cause of events;

H_i is one of a set of n mutually exclusive hypotheses;

$P(H_i)$ is the starting, or "prior" probability of an hypothesis;

$P(E|H_i)$ is the probability of an event occurring given the prior probability of H_i.

$P(H_i|E)$ is the revised probability of H_i given that event E has already occurred.

In words, it says that, given an analyst's starting probabilities $P(H_i)$—his intuitive feeling for the likelihoods of a set of more or less mutually exclusive hypotheses—and given his assessments $P(E|H_i)$—how likely an event would be if each of the hypotheses were true—the updated probability of the hypotheses themselves—$P(H_i|E)$—can be calculated in a straightforward fashion. The procedure is also recursive; if there is more than one event to be assessed, the updated or revised probabilities of the hypotheses from this round become the starting probabilities for the next round.

The example which was given previously is shown here calculated in full, using the Bayesian formula:

$$P(H_1) = .1$$

$$P(H_2) = .9$$

$$P(E|H_1) = .99$$

$$P(E|H_2) = .8$$

$$P(H_1|E) = \frac{P(H_1) \times P(E|H_1)}{\sum_{i=1}^{2}[P(H_i) \times P(E|H_i)]} = \frac{.1 \times .99}{.099 + .72} = \frac{.099}{.819} = .12$$

$$P(H_2|E) = \frac{P(H_2) \times P(E|H_2)}{\sum_{i=1}^{2}[P(H_i) \times P(E|H_i)]} = \frac{.9 \times .8}{.099 + .72} = \frac{.72}{.819} = .88$$

Appendix 2:
Limitations of the Method

Limited Applicability

The first and foremost reservation in the use of this technique, as noted earlier, is that it is applicable only to certain types of questions. They must be capable of definition as a set of fairly distinct outcomes or hypotheses. Also, the present procedure involving many analysts, cartographic plates, and finished printing is too cumbersome to use on crisis questions. It is certainly possible, however, for the technique to be further adapted, either through computer assistance in routing and printing, or by eliminating the printing overhead and the complexity of operating with many analysts.

Data Problems

There is the problem of identifying which evidence is relevant, that is, whether certain peripheral items should be included, and if included, whether they should carry less weight than the other items. We have delegated that decision to the analysts. After all, they are the experts, and their frequent disagreement over items shows that objective measures of relevance would be virtually impossible to devise. Very little editorial judgment is imposed by the coordinator in the process of consolidating evidence, and any item that appears to be even marginally related is included for evaluation. Nevertheless, each analyst is then allowed to ignore any item he considers irrelevant. This gives the participants great leeway in what they rate, but insures that they at least see the evidence and make an explicit decision on its relevance. Furthermore, if a participant sees two or more items as overlapping, he is asked to rate only one of them.

Related to this is the problem of source reliability. A report may come from an unreliable source, it may be subject to other interpretations, or it may be a misleading fabrication. Although some methodologists have suggested that each analyst assign a numerical measure of source reliability along with each item, to be incorporated into the calculations as a weight, we have avoided placing this extra burden on the analyst by requesting that he internalize this requirement and assign probabilities that reflect how much faith he places in each item. If an analyst understands the process and rates items thoughtfully, he can cause items of greater salience and reliability to have a greater effect on the calculations. This is because the effect of an item increases as the range of probabilities assigned to it increases.

Another related problem is that of negative evidence, or "the dog that barked in the nighttime" (from "Silver Blaze," a Sherlock Holmes story in which the singular event was that the dog *did not* bark in the nighttime). This refers to the fact that the absence of any positive evidence may in itself be highly indicative, and the journalistic bias toward reporting events rather than nonevents compounds the situation. That is, we tend to get news only of events or changes, whereas the fact that the status quo is being maintained may be quite significant, and there is no way for the analyst to rate this. We recognize the problem, and feel that it is at least partially solved by including the following item whenever it appears necessary: "How likely is it that only these events would occur (and be seen) if hypothesis one (or two, three, etc.) is true? "

Problems over Time

There are difficulties in the use of the method in a project continuing over many months. First, the questions probably require some reference to a time period (explicit or implicit) in which the hypotheses are to manifest themselves. That is, whether they will occur within thirty days or a year or five years. As a project such as this continues, the time frame must either contract or move forward. Contraction would occur if there is a fixed date in the future which limits the possibilities, such as the development of a nuclear potential by 1978. In this case, the passage of time and the reduction of the period remaining may itself be of significance, and a coordinator may choose to include an item to that effect for evaluation. Moving the time frame forward occurs when the question is of the probability of events within the next thirty days, etc. This is looking through a "sliding window," and the approach raises the problem of retaining or discarding data that was evaluated months earlier with regard to an earlier frame of possibilities. Our solution has been to drop earlier evaluations and recalculate the probabilities each time using only a fixed time span of evidence multiplied against the original intuitive probabilities. The intuitive starting probabilities are also updated at intervals.

Problems with Numbers

There are also two numerical problems. The first is that a probability of zero is mathematically, not to mention analytically, unacceptable. If any conditional probability is evaluated at zero, the probability of the related hypothesis becomes zero, and no amount of other evidence can rejuvenate the probability. Thus, any evaluation of zero should be replaced by a very small number. The second, and more profound, problem is the way individual analysts handle probabilities. It has been our experience that some people think easily in probabilities, others have to work at it every time, and a few need constant attention and retraining to overcome a distorted or unrealistic feeling for probabilities. The only solution for this problem, aside from a careful initial choice and subsequent replacement of analysts, is constant attention to the analysts' assessments and frequent retraining using illustrative items of evidence.

Manipulation

Finally, there is the problem of conscious manipulation. An analyst may assign his probabilities in a manner that reflects a predetermined goal rather than unbiased judgment. Although we have found this to be quite rare, nevertheless it does occur. In our early studies, the participants were identified with the Bayesian trend lines, and there were occasions of manipulation. Avoiding disciplinary solutions, we have almost entirely circumvented the problem by identifying the participants on the supplementary intuitive graphs and not on the Bayesian charts. This allows them to express strongly held personal opinions in a forum designed for that purpose, and the validity of the Bayesian calculations is greatly enhanced.

3

Cross-Impact Analysis: Forecasting the Future of Rhodesia

Frank Moritz

A highly successful test application of cross-impact analysis was carried out in the spring of 1976. This report describes the method itself and how it was used, and projects the future utility we foresee for the use of cross-impact analysis as an intelligence tool.

Of all the methodological issues facing the political forecaster, the problem of the linkage between events is one of the hardest with which to deal. In the complex problems of greatest interest to policymakers, everything seems to be related to everything else, so that the occurrence of any one event invariably depends upon whether a number of other events do or do not occur. It is extremely difficult, because of this, to single out one event and to forecast with any degree of precision the probability of its occurrence.

Cross-impact analysis is a forecasting tool which permits one to deal with the problem that "everything is related to everything else" by systematically examining how any particular event affects the likelihood of all other events to which it is judged to be related in a particular problem

An earlier version of this paper, entitled "Cross-Impact Analysis for Intelligence Forecasting," was presented at the Eighteenth Annual Convention of the International Studies Association, held in St. Louis, March 1977.

context. Two components are central to the cross-impact process: (1) subjective expert judgment, to estimate the relationship or impact between each of the related events in a problem; and (2) a computer or some other dispassionate bookkeeping device, to make sure that no information is lost and to calculate a truly logical summary of these judgmental decisions. In addition to being procedurally thorough and quantitatively precise, the process generates a set of data that can be manipulated to study the impact of a wide range of alternative futures concerning the problem at hand—that is, it permits one to ask "what if" questions.

Although the greatest "consumer" attention is most often focused on the conclusion of a forecast, from a substantive point of view the really crucial element of any such estimate lies in the process by which the underlying assumptions are specified, assessed, and summed into a logical conclusion. The cross-impact technique was judged a potentially useful tool for intelligence and other policy-related analysis, because it provides a clear structure for managing the forecasting process, and because it requires that all assumptions which go into a forecast be clearly articulated. Thus, any conclusions reached through this technique can be both defended and critiqued by tracing the analytical argument back through a visible path of underlying premises.

The results of a cross-impact process are also rendered in a manner which permits them to be employed in a variety of useful ways: (1) The quantitatively stated relationships found or assumed to exist among a set of related events yield patterns that can be translated into logically defensible scenarios or alternative futures. (2) The pattern of relationships defined in a cross-impact exercise constitutes a model whose component elements can be altered and manipulated to study the consequences of future events other than those judged to be most likely. (3) Once the technique has been applied to a particular problem, it can easily be used to assure that subsequent estimates of the problem are updated in a way that is sufficiently consistent to permit valid comparisons among estimates.

Although the computational techniques used in cross-impact analysis are complex, the concepts underlying them are not. Suppose that a set of developments related to a particular problem or issue is foreseen as possibly occurring by some defined date. The probability of each individual event occurring may vary along a spectrum from virtual certainty to near-impossibility, but the common feature shared among them is that the occurrence of any of them would have some perceived impact or effect upon the overall problem. Once a full set of events related to the problem is specified and their individual probabilities of occurrence are estimated, then the question is posed: "If (e.g., Event 1) occurs, how does that affect or change the probabilities of each of the other related events?" In other words, we speak of a cross-impact effect if the probability of one event varies either positively or negatively with the occurrence or nonoccurrence of other events. The initial probabilities for each event and all of the conditional probabilities are arranged in a "cross-impact matrix" that is then analyzed by computer.

As is the case in most substantive applications of a methodological approach, the practical utility of the method depends as much on a smooth-running set of procedural arrangements which facilitate analytical discussion and judgment, as it does on the computational leverage of arcane formulae. Thus, it may help the reader to get a better intuitive feel for what a cross-impact analysis actually does if we outline below the major steps in the process.

When a topic for analysis has been decided, and a group of analysts knowledgeable on that subject has been assembled, the group will begin (1) by deciding upon a reporting time frame that is relevant to policy needs or other interests, and (2) by enumerating a list of events or developments which could possibly occur within the time frame, and whose occurrence would have some effect on the issue being studied. (In our test, the major issue was the Rhodesian situation in early 1976 and the time projection was one year. The list of events which analysts judged might occur during this time period is shown in Table 1, p. 39.) The group of analysts is next asked to estimate, for each event, the probability of that event occurring within the established time frame. This can cover both the occurrence and nonoccurrence of events. If nonoccurrence is considered relevant or salient for only a few of them, it would be easiest to add events in a negative form (e.g., Event 3 is not going to take place in the next x years). When this first step is completed, the coordinator of the exercise arranges the set of events in a matrix format.

Using the matrix as a guide, the group next decides on the conditional probabilities for each paired set of events in the matrix. That is, they are asked to use the matrix to estimate how (if at all) each event's occurrence would affect the original probabilities of every other event in the set. For example: "If Event 1 occurred, what then would be the probability of Event 2 occurring, of Event 3 occurring, etc.?" Figure 1 illustrates this process by showing the initial probabilities and the conditional probabilities in the cross-impact matrix for five of the seventeen events included in the Rhodesian test case. It will be seen that the matrix serves as a model of analysts' perceptions and judgments on the Rhodesian issue. The values in each of the cells of the matrix are judgmental inputs, any number of which may be revised to reflect changes in perceptions or real world events. When all of the conditional probabilities have been estimated, they are entered into the computer as the basic information which

FIGURE 1

EXAMPLE OF CROSS-IMPACT MATRIX

EVENT	INITIAL PROBABILITY
1. Increased Rhodesian operations into Mozambique	50%
2. Major increase of Soviet assistance to insurgents	40%
3. Outbreak of urban terrorism in Rhodesia	5%
4. South African pressure on Rhodesia to negotiate	15%
5. Achievement of a unified insurgent military effort	10%

INITIAL PROBABILITY

	E1 .50	E2 .40	E3 .05	E4 .15	E5 .10
If this event occurs:	Then the above probabilities become:				
E1 Increased Rhodesian operations into Mozambique	–	70	.05	.25	.15
E2 Major increase of Soviet assistance to insurgents	.20	–	.20	.50	.25
E3 Outbreak of urban terrorism in Rhodesia	.05	.40	–	.25	.05
E4 South African pressure on Rhodesia to negotiate	30	.40	.05	–	.10
E5 Achievement of a unified insurgent military effort	30	.80	.40	.75	–

will be used as alternative futures for the issue are explored in subsequent runs through the cross-impact process.

The cross-impact computer program employs a Monte Carlo procedure in tracing out the cross-impacts to arrive at a revised initial probability for each of the events. A first event is selected (either randomly or as specified by the analyst) and is then subjected to a random decision, based on its probability, as to whether it does or does not occur. Using the previously established conditional probabilities, the probabilities of the remaining events are then adjusted to reflect the occurrence or nonoccurrence of the first event. A second event is then "decided," and the probabilities of the remaining events are again adjusted to reflect the occurrence or nonoccurrence of this event. When all events in the set have been decided, this represents one complete "play" of the matrix. The computer plays the matrix in this manner at least 1,200 times, so that revised probabilities can be computed on the basis of the percentage of times that an event occurs during these plays. All of these quantitative operations are performed by computer, with no technical burden placed upon the group of substantive analysts.

The initial probabilities and the matrix of conditional probabilities provides a data base which permits at least three kinds of analysis. First, one checks the logical consistency of the probabilities assigned by the analysts. The initial computer output is a revised probability for each event derived by tracing all the cross-impacts of each event on all other events. This is a logical extrapolation of the judgments made by the analysts. When this revised probability differs significantly from the initial intuitive probability judgments, as was the case in our Rhodesian test case, the reasons for this difference can be identified by tracing the cross-impacts through the matrix to identify those which had not been taken into account in the initial intuitive judgment. The analyst then has two options. He may conclude, on the basis of this new insight, that his initial probability judgment was incorrect, or he may stick with this judgment and revise his conditional (cross-impact) probabilities to make them consistent with his initial probability judgment. The virtue of the procedure is that it identifies these logical inconsistencies and raises new questions, not that it necessarily produces a "right" answer.

A second way of manipulating the data is for sensitivity analysis. It is possible to determine how a change in the probability of occurrence of one event would, through its cross-impacts, affect the probability of all other events. When analysts disagree on a probability judgment, the program can be run using these alternative judgments to determine how much difference this disagreement really makes on the probability of the other events. One can also conduct a systematic analysis to identify which events would trigger the greatest impact on the system. To do this, the program is run many times, changing the probability of only one event for each running. The probability of each event is set first at 1, to indicate the event has occurred, and then at 0, to indicate the event will not occur. The impact of these changes on the probability of all other events is readily apparent from the computer output. This type of analysis might be used, for example, to test the potential impact of policy decisions, to update an estimate when some real world event actually does occur, or to identify which variables are most critical to the system and, therefore, may require further research or monitoring.

The third kind of analysis is the testing of scenarios. By setting a series of events at 1 or 0, to indicate occurrence or nonoccurrence, one can build a variety of scenarios and test their impact on outcome events. It is possible, in this way, to determine how the probability of some specified outcome varies, depending upon alternative scenarios specifying the occurrence or nonoccurrence of a number of related events.

Clearly, the results of cross-impact analysis are an artifact of the judgments originally supplied when estimating the initial cross-impact probabilities. Nevertheless, the method permits systematic collation of judgment and makes explicit the sometimes hidden effects of multiple linkages between events.

The Test Exercise

To test the application of the cross-impact technique, we contracted with the Futures Group, Inc., to purchase a copy of the computer program which is central to this process, and to obtain the personal advice and assistance of their cross-impact specialists. The Futures Group has been the leading developer of this forecasting approach (largely for corporate planning purposes thus far), and their advice was considered indispensable in determining how to adapt the method for intelligence purposes. (For a bibliography on cross-impact analysis, see Wayne I. Boucher and John Stover, *An Annotated Bibliography of Cross-Impact Analysis* [Glastonburg, Conn.: The Futures Group, 1976]).

Once the program was working properly on the Agency's computer system, it was decided to use the Rhodesian situation as our test case. Southern Africa had been the subject of a recent National Intelligence Estimate, in which an extensive set of scenarios was elaborated to depict alternative future outcomes in that area of the world. Thus, we were able to test, by comparison, the ability of the cross-impact method to help generate scenarios. A panel of participants was assembled and the exercise took place during the week of 26-30 April 1976. Although the Rhodesian situation changed dramatically several months after this exercise, and the

TABLE 1

EVENT	INITIAL PROBABILITY (assigned by analysts)
1. Expansion of insurgency from Mozambique	85%
2. Increased Rhodesian operations into Mozambique	50%
3. Opening of insurgency on Zambian border	45%
4. Significant African participation in insurgency	10%
5. Significantly increased Communist assistance to insurgents	40%
6. Interdiction of rail transportation between Rhodesia and South Africa	15%
7. S.A. pressure on Rhodesia to force negotiations	15%
8. S.A. military intervention into Rhodesia to support Rhodesia	5%
9. Urban terrorism in Rhodesia	5%
10. Opening of negotiations in Rhodesia	5%
11. Achievement of negotiated settlement in Rhodesia	1%
12. Communist military involvement inside Rhodesia	5%
13. Increased level of hostilities due to economic factors	10%
14. Decreased level of hostilities due to economic factors	10%
15. British offer of bail-out for Rhodesia	30%
16. Achievement of unified insurgent military effort	10%
17. Significant increased Chinese assistance to insurgents	30%

analysts took only a preliminary cut at the problem on this occasion, the exercise is still illustrative of how the method works.

The participants began the first session by deciding upon a list of events whose occurrence during the next twelve months (however unlikely at that time) would have a qualitative impact on the overall situation in Rhodesia. The seventeen events shown in Table 1 were chosen as representing the major developments that could take place within a year.

The analysts assigned an initial probability to each event, i.e., they made a numerical guess of the likelihood that each event, (considered independently) would occur within twelve months. There was, surprisingly, little disagreement about the general range within which each estimate fell, and consensus was quickly reached on all seventeen probabilities.

The group of analysts then began the task of filling in a cross-impact matrix by deciding how the occurrence of each event would change the initially estimated probability of every other event. Between 1000 and 1200 hours on the first day's session, the participants filled in all the cells in the first five horizontal rows of the matrix—a very good pace considering that substantive debate preceded the group's decision for each of these initial 85 (5 x 17) cross-impacts. At this point the coordinator decided that, rather than schedule a second group meeting to finish the matrix, each of the analysts should take his own worksheet, fill in the cross-impacted cells, and return it to the coordinator, who would compile a composite matrix.

This latter step was a departure from usual procedure in cross-impact, but it was a necessary test of the method's flexibility under the time constraints of the normal intelligence process. The participants all completed their worksheets by the end of the next day, with surprisingly few major disagreements over the individual cross-impacts, and a completed matrix was assembled for computer processing. The initial analysis of the data was done by the experienced consultants at the Futures Group.

A follow-up meeting was held on April 30, at which the analytical results were presented to the participants and to office management. The expertise of our consultants was essential on this point, since the interpretation of the numerical results is perhaps the most critical, yet least straightforward, step of the cross-impact analysis process. The readouts which follow below represent, in quantitative form, the computed implications of the assumptions which our group of analysts specified in the original cross-impact matrix.

Impact of Initial Computer
Run on Event Probabilities

Only events whose probabilities increased or decreased measurably are included below.

For Event 4, significant African participation in insurgency, the initial probability of 0.10 was raised to 0.30 as a result of the incremental effect of Events 2, 3, 6, 8, 12, 13, and 16. These events include local and regional escalation, and external intervention, particularly by South Africa; they have the effect of galvanizing other African states into active participation.

For Event 5, significant increase in communist assistance to insurgents, the initial probability of 0.40 was raised to 0.70 as a result of substantial impacts of Events 1, 2, 3, 4, 6, 8, 12, 13, and 17. These events include an intensification and broadening of the conflict, including in particular, direct South African and communist troop intervention, and an increase in fighting due to economic costs. These events increase the insurgents' need for external assistance.

For Event 6, complete interdiction, due to insurgency, of Rhodesian rail connections with South Africa, the initial probability of 0.05 was raised to 0.30 as a result of incremental impacts of Events 1, 3, 5, 9, 12, and 16. These events include general intensification and broadening of the conflict, the opening of urban guerrilla warfare in Rhodesia, and achievement of a unified insurgency. A unified insurgency and communist troop involvement, by enhancing the insurgents' capabilities, have the greatest impacts.

For Event 7, South African pressure on Rhodesia to negotiate with insurgents, the initial probability of 0.15 was raised to 0.55 as a result of substantial impacts of Events 2, 3, 4, 5, 6, 9, 12, 15, and 16. These events all involve the risk or actuality of a broadened conflict and enhanced insurgency capabilities. The exception is the United Kingdom bail-out, which has the greatest influence on Event 7 of any other single event. Presumably, these events in the aggregate increase the risks to South Africa from continued conflict, and perhaps offer a reasonable alternative—white resettlement—to continued conflict.

For Event 9, urban guerrilla warfare begins in Rhodesia, the initial probability of 0.05 was raised to 0.20 as a result of cumulative impacts of Events 1, 3, 8, 12, and 16. These events involve a broadening of the conflict to include South African and communist troops and most importantly, the achievement of a unified guerrilla movement. These events have the effect of enhancing both the incentives and the capabilities for urban guerrilla warfare.

For Event 10, negotiations open between Smith and Rhodesian insurgents, the initial probability of 0.05 was raised to 0.50 as a result of substantial impacts of Events 6, 7, 12 and incremental impacts of Events 5, 15, and 16. These events include, most importantly, increased external and internal military activity against the Rhodesian government, and South African pressure on the Smith regime for negotiations. These combined sources of pressure further isolate the Rhodesian whites and increase inducements to negotiate.

For Event 11, negotiations succeed, the initial probability of 0.01 was raised to 0.40 as a result of substantial effects of Events 6, 7, 9, 10, and 16. These events include increased internal military activity against the Smith regime continuing during negotiations, South African pressure on Smith to negotiate, the United Kingdom bail-out offer, and the opening of negotiations themselves. These events increase internal and external pressure on the Rhodesian government to negotiate in good faith.

For Event 12, significant communist (Cuban) troop involvement in Rhodesia, the initial probability of 0.05 was raised to 0.30 as a result of substantial effects of Events 2, 5, and 8. These events include, most importantly, Rhodesian escalation and South African intervention, which increase the need and opportunity for communist troops.

For Event 15, United Kingdom offers Rhodesia a bail-out, the initial probability of 0.30 was raised to 0.60 as a result of substantial effects of all events except 2, 14, and 17. These events include both a general increase in the intensity and breadth of conflict, and the opening of successful negotiations.

For Event 17, significant increase in Communist Chinese material and advisory assistance, the initial probability of 0.30 was raised to 0.60 as a result of substantial impacts of Events 2, 3, 4, 5, 6, 8, and 13. These events include a general intensification of military conflict, external—particularly South African—participation, and increased conflict due to economic costs, but do not include communist troop involvement. These events increase the need and opportunity for Communist Chinese assistance.

Those familiar with the southern African situation will be surprised to note the increased probability of the "negotiated settlement" scenario (Event 11). This turned out to be the computer's way of showing us that a greater number of "outcome" events should have been specified: i.e., as the impacts multiplied through the matrix, the only natural end point toward which they could fall was the outcome of a negotiated settlement. This fact, however, demonstrated a strength rather than a shortcoming of the technique. The process is supposed to be iterative, allowing the users to build a better model of the problem situation, as well as to generate alternative outcomes.

Conclusions and Future Work

The response of the participants was very favorable, as evidenced by the fact that several of them requested follow-up runs on a matrix that takes account of their divergences from group consensus on particular points. Everyone involved in this test exercise tended to agree that, regardless of the numerical outcomes, the educational process involved in debating each cross-impact was invaluable. For this reason, the technique would seem to be a useful tool that could be applied by a group or an individual at some point in any estimative study.

In general, we were impressed most by the education and learning process which the participants experienced while deciding upon their cross-impact estimates. This technique leads analysts to use their full potential, because it requires them to articulate their assumptions explicitly and to examine the consistency of those assumptions. The discipline involved in the selection of items, and particularly the systematic questioning necessary to establish cross-impacts, was often enlightening. The analysts were asked to decide what events might be important and how they might affect one another. This confrontation often illustrated that issues once believed to be simple and independent were, in reality, interrelated. Simply completing the matrix forced enough introspection to be useful; and, of course, the mathematical play of the basic matrix, using new initial conditions to simulate policies or less likely courses of events, showed unexpected secondary and tertiary consequences of these developments or policy choices.

In using cross-impact techniques, we sought to find what we have called the "conditional probabilities" of forecasted items in a set, in full consideration of the potential interactions among all of them. The systematic description of all potential interactions and the assessment of the possible strength of these interactions is complex but methodologically important, since the combination of these descriptions and clearly stated assumptions may provide new insight into past events, and also permit greater accuracy and precision in forecasting. A well-adapted use of the cross-impact approach for intelligence would almost certainly permit the exploration of the side effects of decisions under consideration. It might also be useful to illuminate less expensive means of serving intelligence needs by investment in high-payoff areas which initially seem unrelated or only weakly linked to certain policy concerns. From an intelligence point of view, it could also help to target previously neglected areas of analysis, the study of which might yield more complete explanations of a larger problem.

4
Regression Analysis: Impact of Economic Conditions on Left Voting in France

Susan Koch and Fred Grupp

The Problem

To what extent is popular support for the French Left related to domestic economic conditions? Many observers, including President Valéry Giscard d'Estaing and Prime Minister Raymond Barre, have expressed the belief that popular economic dissatisfaction increases the appeal of the Socialist and Communist parties. Others, especially but not exclusively members of the French Left, hold the contrary view that an economic upturn would actually raise the Left's electoral chances, since a new and different government would seem less risky during a more prosperous period. Still others, including perhaps Gaullist leader Jacques Chirac, claim that there is no strong relationship between economic conditions and voting, that the electorate is motivated primarily by political considerations.

Hypotheses about the impact of economic conditions on French voting thus abound, but the question has not been the object of much systematic study.[1] In an effort to resolve this question, we tested the various prevailing hypotheses empirically through a long-term analysis of the relationship between selected aggregate economic indicators and voting for Left parties in France. Our work was stimulated and con-

TABLE 1

PARTIES INCLUDED IN "LEFT" GROUPING

Election	Parties
1927	Communists, Socialists, Independent Socialists, Social Republicans, Radicals, Independent Radicals
1928	Communists, Socialists, Miscellaneous Left, Independent Socialists, Republican Socialists, Radical Socialists
1932	Communists, Socialists, Miscellaneous Left, Republican Socialists, Radical Socialists
1936	Communists, Miscellaneous Left, Socialists, Radical Socialists
October 1945, June 1946, November 1946	Communists, Socialists, Radical Socialists, Rally of the Republican Left, Democratic and Socialist Union of the Resistance
1951, 1956	Communists, Miscellaneous Left, Socialists, Radical Socialists, Rally of the Republican Left, Democratic and Socialist Union of the Resistance
1958	Communists, Union of Democratic Forces, Socialists, Radical Socialists
1962	Communists, Far Left, Socialists, Radical Socialists
1967	Communists, Far Left, Left Federation
1968	Communists, Unified Socialist Party, Left Federation, Miscellaneous Left
1973	Communists, Unified Socialist Party, Far Left, Union of the Democratic and Socialist Left, Miscellaneous Left

siderably aided by that of Jean-Jacques Rosa and Daniel Amson, which examined the relationship between votes for the Left in French legislative elections from 1924 to 1973, and the per capita income, unemployment and price levels of the year preceding each election.[2] Table 1 lists the parties which they—and we—group under the heading "Left." The inclusion of the Radicals, who became progressively more conservative during the period studied, overstates the Left's vote in the early postwar elections, but does not seriously skew the findings for the most recent years, when the Radical votes declined greatly. Only the Left Radicals, who by then had joined the Socialist-Communist coalition, are included in the Left grouping for the 1973 election.

Rosa and Amson studied the relationship between economic conditions and electoral results over the entire fifty-year period and found statistically significant correlations, but they ignored the very real possibility of dramatic changes in the relationships between variables within that time frame. If the relationships between economic indicators and Left voting wax and wane, or even reverse signs, then the regression analysis based on those correlations will be less effective in explaining voting patterns. We examined Rosa and Amson's data, therefore, not only for changes in relationship between the independent economic variables and Left voting, but also for changes between the economic indicators, such as inflation and unemployment, themselves. Those relationships are displayed graphically in Figure 1.

It is also important to note that we did not inquire into the factors motivating the stable core of Left voters. Our interest was in the impact of economic conditions on the change in the vote for the Left from one election to another.

Figure 1

Economic Conditions and Votes for the French Left, 1923-1973

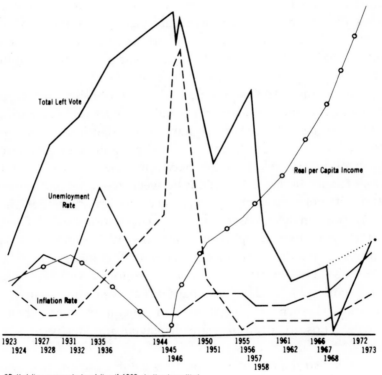

*Dotted line represents trend line if 1968 election is omitted

The Findings

Our working hypothesis argued that Left voting would rise dramatically during a serious depression, decrease during prosperity, and increase slightly during a recession. In fact, the relationship between economic conditions and votes for the Left proved to be considerably more complex and interesting, as shown in Figure 1.[3] It basically depended on the relative salience of the political and economic environments at the time of each election. For most of the period, political concerns were paramount; since the early 1960s, economic issues have come to the fore.

Before 1962, there was no consistent relationship between French economic conditions and electoral support for the Left. During the interwar period, the economic situation had a strong electoral impact only in 1936, after the world economic crisis had hit France. In that year, economic dissatisfaction was sufficiently great to be felt at the ballot box, even though major political issues were also at stake in the election. Support for the Left—specifically for the Communist part (PCF)—grew as income fell and unemployment and inflation rose. Radical and Socialist votes, on the other hand, were inversely correlated with severe economic discontent; they increased during the relative prosperity of the 1920s and early 1930s, and fell in 1936.

The relationship between economic conditions and voting behavior was even less clear between 1945 and 1962. During that period, economic considerations were overshadowed by major political issues. The experience of World War II and the Resistance benefitted the Socialists and Communists. The Cold War hurt the PCF. The Indochinese and Algerian conflicts probably both hurt and helped the Left. The appeal of Mendes-France increased support for the Radicals in the mid-1950s. The fall of the Fourth Republic and creation of the

Fifth hurt the Socialists, Communists, and Radicals, all of whom lost votes to the revitalized Gaullist party.

After 1962, those overriding political factors were considerably muted or had entirely disappeared. East-West tension was giving way to détente; the Fifth Republic was firmly established; the Algerian War was ended. Since there was internal and external political calm, economic considerations could finally have a consistent and important electoral impact. If we discount the election of June 1968, Left votes, inflation, unemployment and per capita income are closely intercorrelated for the legislative elections between 1962 and 1973. Left votes rose along with each of our three economic indicators.

If 1968 is not included, there are only three legislative contests between 1962 and 1973. In order to increase statistical reliability, we added the two presidential elections in which there was a viable Left candidate (those of 1965 and 1974) to the data. The correlations among the three economic indicators and votes for the Left continued to be extremely high, as shown in Table 2, suggesting that a significant trend was at work.

One might argue that the increase in votes for the Left after 1962 had less to do with economic factors than with the general bipolarization of French politics—that is, the disappearance of the Center and the emergence of two competing electoral coalitions on the Left and Right. The shift of support away from the Center and other minor parties may in fact have been largely the product of noneconomic factors, but the choice of the Left by increasing numbers of voters appears to have been very strongly influenced by economic considerations. Otherwise, the correlations between the economic indicators and voters for the Left would almost certainly not be so high.

The relationship between economic conditions and votes

TABLE 2

MATRIX OF INTERCORRELATIONS AMONG ECONOMIC VARIABLES AND VOTES FOR THE LEFT

1. Inflation rate	1.0				(.918)*
2. Per capita national income index	.953	1.0			(.028)
3. Unemployment rate	.968	.970	1.0	(2.37)
4. Votes for Left	.952	.928	.991	1.0

*The unstandardized regression coefficients derived from simple regression of Left voting on each economic indicator are presented in parentheses.

for the Left that prevailed in 1962, 1964, and 1967 was not observed in 1968, and for good reason. The June 1968 elections occurred at a time when French political and economic life had been brought to a standstill by a month of disruptive strikes and demonstrations, with total collapse perceived as a real possibility. In 1973, when all was quiet again, the pattern established between 1962 and 1967 reappeared.

That pattern is different from the one observed in 1936. Between 1962 and 1973, votes for the Left in legislative elections increased along with inflation and unemployment, but they did so at a time when real per capita income was dramatically rising, rather than falling. Recent increases in Left votes, therefore, apparently resulted not from complete economic dissatisfaction, but from discontent with the gaps in a generally prosperous system. Current survey data, and our own predictive model based on the relationship observed between 1962 and 1973 in Figure 1, indicate that the recession which began after the quadrupling of oil prices in 1973 has not diminished support for the Left. On the contrary, the dramatic growth in inflation and unemployment have convinced many voters to switch to the Left. Per capita income growth has not slackened so much as to frighten many into a more conservative position.

Because they are relatively prosperous, voters who switch to the Left in France today are probably less radical than voters in 1936. In that year, the Socialist vote declined slightly, while that of the PCF—and of the Left as a whole—rose. Since 1973, the situation has been reversed. The Socialists, and therefore the Left as a whole, have gained while the PCF has lost. But even if a majority of the new Left voters are not radicals, they still want real change. The Socialists did not start gaining simultaneously with Communist decline until after 1969, when the old middle-of-the-road Socialist party (the *Section Française de l'Internationale Ouvrière*) was replaced by the more leftist *Parti Socialiste*.

The general economic and political conditions which have been observed in France since 1962 have been characteristic of many advanced industrial countries. The internal and external political environment is generally quiet. During the prosperous 1960s and early 1970s, many countries experienced higher unemployment and inflation along with rapid economic growth. Inflation was often considered an inevitable by-product of rapid growth, while some parts of the population found themselves with outmoded, and therefore unemployable, skills in the wake of overall expansion. Unemployment and inflation were generally kept to low, politically acceptable levels until the 1975 recession, but they did exist. And, at least in France, their political impact has remained constant.

Since 1962, higher inflation and unemployment have increased electoral support for the Left. The recent upsurge in prices and the number of unemployed has simply meant a more pronounced shift of voters to the Left. Rising income,

inflation and unemployment might not have the same electoral impact in other industrial states, but since their political
and economic environments have been broadly similar to
France's, the issue merits examination.

A Forecasting Model

The strength of the relationship between the economic
indicators and votes for the Left in France led us to try to
develop an electoral forecasting model based on it. The extremely high intercorrelations among the economic indicators
posed a problem, since any multivariate coefficients generated by the model would inevitably be unstable. If there was
a statistical problem in using multiple regression analysis,
however, there was an intellectual problem in not doing so.
Inflation, unemployment and income levels are conceptually
distinct; they are neither alternate measures of the same
economic phenomenon nor politically similar in their consequences. It was necessary, therefore, to include the electoral
effects of change in all three economic conditions in any
predictive model.

Our solution was simply to add together the electoral
impact of each of the three economic variables. This ignored
any overlapping political impact that the economic indicators
might have, but the success of our "postdicting" efforts suggests that such overlap is minimal. The formula for our model
is:

$$X = Y + (U_{x-1} - U_{y-1})r^U + (I_{x-1} - I_{y-1})r^I + (P_{x-1} - P_{y-1})r^P$$

where X = Left vote in election that one wishes to predict
  Y = Left vote in previous election of same type
  (legislative or presidential)

U = Percentage of unemployed in labor force
I = Annual growth in per capita national income
P = Annual inflation rate
$x\text{-}1$ = Year before the election X
$y\text{-}1$ = Year before the election Y
r^U, r^I, r^P = the unstandardized regression coefficients for unemployment, per capita income growth and inflation respectively, generated by the regression analysis of the five legislative and presidential elections between 1962 and 1974.

We used the model to "postdict" each of the national elections between 1962 and 1974, with accurate results as shown in Table 3. Unfortunately, no similarly successful projection of the 1978 legislative elections could be expected at the time of writing (fall 1977). In the first place, we would have to rely on estimates of the three economic indicators, rather than actual values. More importantly, political factors could emerge which would dilute, neutralize, or even negate the electoral effect of economic conditions.

At least one extraneous political factor already seemed likely to counteract the power of economic determinants of voter choice. Negotiations among the three Left parties on updating their Common Program of Government broke down in late September 1977, leading to the widespread expectation that their coalition will split apart—if not before, then shortly after, the elections. Many voters, who would have supported the Left for economic reasons, will probably turn away from it in disillusionment at its apparent inability to maintain a viable potential governing team when it was so close to victory.

Conversely, in the event that the Left coalition does manage to convince the electorate that it would form a stable government, some voters who would have shifted to the Left

TABLE 3

FRENCH ELECTION RESULTS
(First Round Results in Percentages)

	Actual Left Vote	Predicted Left Vote	Difference
1962 Legislatives	44.4	43.3	−1.1
1965 Presidentials	45.0	45.3	+0.3
1967 Legislatives	45.1	45.8	+0.7
1973 Legislatives	46.7	48.1	+1.4
1974 Presidentials	49.0	48.4	−0.6

for reasons of economic dissatisfaction may not actually do so because of their unwillingness to see Communists participate in the government.

If these or other political developments do not override the impact of the economic variables, and if 1977 sees 2.5 percent per capita income growth, 9.5 percent inflation and 5.7 percent unemployment, our model would predict that the Socialist-Communist-Left Radical coalition would win 57.8 percent of the national vote. If the coalition recaptures its unified image before the election, that figure would probably be two or three percentage points too high, because of the anti-communism of some potential Left voters. In the more likely event that the Left coalition does not have such a unified image at the time of the election, this forecast would probably be even further from the mark.

Economic conditions can have a clear impact on voting only in the absence of important political considerations. The domestic political factors affecting the 1978 election were not likely to be as powerful as those of 1968, but they will probably still be strong enough to make the results quite different from what our purely economic model would predict.

Notes

1. Much of the research on postwar European electorates has examined the relationship between social class and party choice. See, for example, Otto Kirchheimer, "The Transformation of Western European Party Systems," in Joseph LaPalombara and Myron Weiner, eds., *Political Parties and Political Development* (Princeton: Princeton University Press, 1966), pp. 177-200.

This emphasis on the politics of social class differs considerably, of course, from our reliance on economic conditions as predictors of voter behavior. For a critique of the Kirchheimer thesis and a recent review of work in this area, see Alan Zuckerman and Mark Irving Lichbach, "Stability and Change in European Electorates," *World Politics,* 29 (1977): 523-551.

2. Jean-Jacques Rosa and Daniel Amson, "Conditions économiques et élections: Une analyse politico-économétrique (1920-1973)," *Revue Française de science politique,* 26 (December 1976) 1101-1124. One of the objectives of their research was to see which economic indicators, measured at varying lengths of time from the date of the election, were the most explanatory of Left voting. As did theirs, our research indicated that economic data for the year prior to the election were the most useful.

3. The economic and political variables presented in Figure 1 are drawn according to different scales, in order to present a more easily readable picture of respective trends.

5

Operationalizing a Theoretical Model: Profiles of Violence in Argentina, Ethiopia, and Thailand

Harold E. Dahlgren

I. Introduction

The incidence, as well as the political significance, of civil violence has increased greatly in recent years. In the Western industrial world violence has become a favorite weapon of fanatics and ideologues determined to wrench political change from governments concerned with maintaining established institutions. In the developing world it has become an instrument of mass protest as well as a means of deposing ruling elites unable to cope with mounting social and economic problems. On the international scene it has become a tool of terror and extortion for groups seeking third-country asylum, new political leverage, or a global platform for grievances.

Scholars have suggested various explanations of the use of violence as a political weapon. Some insist on the biological imperative (man's innate aggressiveness), some stress material causes (poverty), others emphasize societal factors (the unresponsiveness of society's institutions), while still others

This is an abridged version of a CIA report entitled *Profile of Violence: An Analytical Model* (PR 76 10025, June 1976). The full report is available from Photoduplication Service, Library of Congress, Washington, D.C. 20540. The full report was also presented at the Eighteenth International Studies Association Annual Convention held in St. Louis, March 16–20 1977.

concentrate on psychological causes (frustration). To the extent the first of these explanations (innate aggressive drives) pertains, it may be assumed to be a relatively unchanging constant in human behavior. The remaining three suggest causal factors which are directly or indirectly dependent upon varying circumstances and conditions of life. Drawing largely on the last two, a theoretical framework developed by Ted Robert Gurr of Northwestern University, which encompasses a combination of socio-psychological and societal factors, has emerged as the dominant theoretical approach in recent years.

In this paper we present a method for applying Gurr's theoretical formulations as an aid in the intelligence analysis of political violence. Our purpose is to develop an analytical tool which can help in systematically assessing the psychological and social motivations which propel groups toward conflict, the capabilities of such groups to engage in political violence, and the intensity and form which such violence might assume in a given situation.

Sections II and III describe the theory developed by Gurr, our derivative model of political violence, and the procedures used in applying it as an analytical aid. Section IV is a report on the results of the first experimental ex post facto application of the model to the precoup situation in Chile in mid-1973, and, thereafter, the results of a second test phase during which the model was applied at monthly intervals to three ongoing situations of political conflict—in Argentina, Ethiopia, and Thailand—in the period November 1974 to June 1975. Section V presents a methodological critique of the model based on these tests. A final section (VI) provides a net assessment of the model's usefulness as an aid in intelligence analysis, and proposes ways in which it might be improved and tailored more closely to intelligence needs.

II. The Theory and the Model

The Gurr theory is based on the well-established proposition that people become frustrated in situations in which their achievements fall short of their expectations.[1] To the extent the discrepancy between achievement and expectations widens, their frustrations or sense of "relative deprivation" (RD) turn into collective anger directed at whatever is perceived to be the frustrating agent. When this is seen to be a political authority, collective anger may turn into political violence. The likelihood of its doing so will depend on two intervening variables: the degree to which the actor group believes that violence is justified, and the extent to which a coercive capability can be brought to bear against the political opponent perceived as the frustrating agent.

In our adaptation of Gurr's theory, the discrepancy between achievement and expectation, or relative deprivation, can arise in three basic areas: with regard to economic conditions, self-improvement and social status, and political participation. Justification of violence can be conceived in two dimensions: the degree to which the actor group believes that resort to violence is sanctioned by doctrinal, moral, or historical precepts (Is it right?), and the extent to which the group's members think violence will *in fact* produce the desired result (Will it work?). The capability to wage violence depends on the ability of the actor group to muster two types of support: coercive force in the form of armed groups or military units, and institutional support in the form of nonviolent psychological, economic, or political pressures. In each case, the capability may be viewed as available from within the actor's own group, from other domestic actors, or from allies outside the country.

The dimensions of the political violence thus generated, i.e., its destructiveness and duration, and the proportion of the community that participates in it, are conceived as the cumulative product of the model's basic variables—relative deprivation (RD), justification, and the two types of capability (coercive force and institutional support). The form the violence takes—turmoil (riots or demonstrations), insurgency (terrorist acts or small-scale guerrilla operations), conspiracy (attempted coups), or internal war (large-scale revolutionary actions or civil war)—depends upon the particular mix of these variables among four types of actor groups: proregime, mass-oriented; proregime, elite-oriented; antiregime, mass-oriented; and antiregime, elite-oriented. The proregime or antiregime characteristic is defined in terms of the group's support for, or opposition to, the existing government. The mass or elite characteristic is defined in terms of the group's primary identification with its general membership or a large mass constituency, on the one hand, or with the policies and ambitions of its leaders, or those of the country's ruling elite, on the other. The specific kinds of groups involved will vary from country to country, and even from time to time within the same country. In all cases, however, the extent to which the model's basic variables are perceived as prevailing among the four types of actor groups will provide the basis for predicting the extent and form of political violence. A graphic representation of the model is shown in Figure 1. The 2 x 2 table in Figure 2 illustrates the four types of actor groups.

III. Constructing the Model

One way to apply the model for our purposes would be to seek "hard" objective data which, on the basis of empirical research or common sense, seem to "represent" the variables and actor characteristics in the model. By developing indica-

Figure 1

A Causal Model of Political Violence

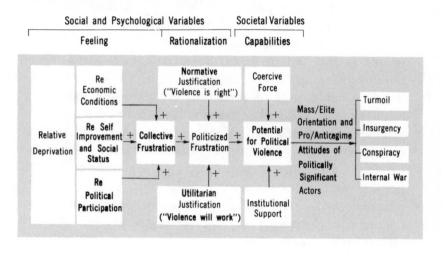

Figure 2

Four Types of Actors in the Model

Actors' Orientation

		MASS	ELITE
Attitude Toward Regime	PRO	Proregime Mass-oriented	Proregime Elite-oriented
	ANTI	Antiregime Mass-oriented	Antiregime Elite-oriented

tors from these data and then tracking them over time against the ebb and flow of political violence in a country, we could arrive at certain conclusions about the model's utility as a predictive tool. Several considerations argue against this approach in the present study, however. "Hard" data on the kind of group actors and essentially subjective socio-psychological variables used in our model are scarce and exceedingly difficult to standardize systematically across countries. To the extent such information does exist, it is available on most countries only for large time periods, normally a year, and would be difficult to disaggregate for the smaller evaluation periods required in the present project. Moreover, objective economic and social data usually apply to a whole country or region rather than to specific actor groups. On all these counts, the problems involved in devising a practical tool from "hard" data to assess current conflict situations of interest to the intelligence analyst would be formidable.

In the present case, therefore, it seemed advisable to turn to "soft," expert-generated data to measure the model's key variables. Indeed, apart from avoiding the above difficulties, several distinct advantages could be expected in the use of intelligence specialists as data sources for the model. In the nature of his work, the intelligence analyst is in a uniquely advantageous position to monitor the behavior of individuals and groups seeking political change through violence. His access to relevant information in this area is presumably greater and more direct than that of his counterparts outside government. Moreover, the kinds of numerical assessments required by the model are not essentially different from those made by the analyst in normal intelligence reports and estimates. Finally, and most importantly, the analyst's day-by-day concentration on selected conflict situations makes it possible to apply the model on a nearly real-time basis, thus enhancing its value as a practical aid to current intelligence production in the policy-making process.

Procedures for Measuring
Variables and Aggregating Data

In this section we describe the procedures used to elicit the requisite data for the model from the intelligence analyst. In the following section we will describe the way the data were aggregated to produce projections of the conditions conducive to particular forms of violence.

First, a panel of five intelligence analysts was selected to assign numerical evaluations to the model's variables for each actor group judged to be a significant political force in the country under observation. The five panelists, representing different components of the Agency, were selected on the basis of their expert knowledge or close observation of various aspects of the country in question.

To simplify analyst evaluations, the main variables of the model—RD, justification, coercive force, and institutional support—were broken down into subcomponents. Each analyst on the five-member panel was given a worksheet (Figure 3) for the assignment of a numerical evaluation to each subcomponent for each politically significant actor in the country under examination. The number and identity of such actors were in each case determined by discussion and consensus among the five panel members.

For the purpose of applying the model, an actor was defined either as a specific political party or movement or as a general special-interest or functional grouping which seemed to exert some systematic influence, pressure, or force either against or on behalf of the existing government to achieve political objectives on a national scale. Under this definition, partisan affiliations were largely ignored. Except for specific

Figure 3

Analyst's Worksheet: Variables

VARIABLES	VARIABLE NUMBER	ACTORS													
		1	2	3	4	5	6	7	8	9	10	11	12	13	60

Social and Psychological Variables

A. Actor's perception of RD re:
1. Economic conditions — 1
2. Self improvement and social status — 2
3. Political participation — 3
4. Total RD or collective frustration (Sum of variables 1, 2, 3) — 4

B. Actor's belief that, to reduce RD, violence is justified:
1. On normative grounds — 5
2. On utilitarian grounds — 6
Total justification (Sum of variables 5 & 6) — 7

Total politicized frustration (Product of variables 4 & 7) — 8

Societal Variables

C. Coercive force available to Actor
1. Within own group — 9
2. From other actors — 10
3. From external allies — 11
Total available coercive force (Sum of variables 9, 10, 11) — 12

D. Institutional support available
1. Within own group — 13
2. From other actors — 14
3. From external allies — 15
Total available institutional support (Sum of variables 13, 14, 15) — 16

Total capability for political violence (Sum of variables 12 & 16) — 17

Potential for political violence (Sum of variables 8 & 17) — 18 political parties or groups, a single actor was conceived as embracing all organizations or movements included in its functional or special-interest category. For some actors, this embraced both progovernment and antigovernment groups. The definition also permitted inclusion of government-affiliated or government-sponsored groups actively engaged in influencing or pressuring nongovernment groups or the general population.

Using the Figure 3 worksheet, each analyst evaluated each actor group (identified by number at the top of each vertical column) on each subcomponent listed in the variable column on the left side of the worksheet. (The subcomponents are numbered 1, 2, 3, 5, 6, 9, 10, 11, 13, 14, and 15.) The analyst scored each of the social and psychological subcomponents (1, 2, 3, 5, and 6) in terms of what he believed the actor's (not his own) perception was of that variable's intensity, the depth of feeling or commitment felt by the actor's members, and scope, the proportion of the actor's members who seemed to share that feeling or commitment. He then scored each of the societal subcomponents (9, 10, 11, 13, 14, and 15) in terms of what he (not the actor) believed was the actual extent of coercive force and institutional support available to the actor in the period under observation. Instructions and a list of questions (Figure 4) were given the analyst to aid him in making his evaluations on each subcomponent.

For each actor the analyst scored each subcomponent on a scale of 0 to 10. A score of 0 meant the subcomponent did not exist for the actor; a score of 10 indicated the subcomponent existed for the actor at a maximum level. In most cases, the analyst was not presumed to have access to concrete data as a basis for his scores. He was expected to rely primarily on his own impressionistic syntheses of whatever information he had accumulated which might shed light

Figure 4.

Questions to Guide the Assignment of Numerical
Evaluations on Key Variables in the Model

In each case, the actor is evaluated *relative to all other actors
on the scene.*

Variable 1: To what extent do members of the actor group
feel frustrated regarding their economic condition and
general welfare? *

Variable 2: To what extent do members of the actor group
feel frustrated regarding their chances for self-improvement
or for gaining increased social status? *

Variable 3: To what extent do members of the actor group
feel frustrated regarding their collective opportunity to
influence or participate in the political process on matters
of concern to them? *

Variable 5: To what extent do members of the actor group
believe that, to relieve their frustrations, violent political
action against the system or opposing actors is justified
on moral, doctrinal, or historical grounds?

Variable 6: To what extent do members of the actor group
believe that, given the practical opportunities and limitations of the current political scene, violent action a-
gainst the system or opposing actors will *in fact* serve to
relieve their frustrations?

Variable 9: To what extent, in terms of equipment, training,
size, strategic location, and loyalty of armed manpower
*available from within their own organization or move-
ment,* are members of the actor group capable of carrying
out political violence?

*In assessing frustrations within the military services, the
primary focus should be on the officer corps but with due
regard for pressures and influences exerted by the rank-and-
file on their superiors.

Figure 4. continued

Variable 10: To what extent, in terms of equipment, train- ing, size, strategic location, and loyalty of armed man- power *available from allied actors within the country,* are members of the actor group capable of carrying out political violence?

Variable 11: To what extent, in terms of equipment, train- ing, size, strategic location, and loyalty of armed manpower *available from allied groups or powers outside the country,* are members of the actor group capable of carrying out political violence?

Variable 13: To what extent, in terms of their organizational cohesion and the size and geographic concentration of their resources, can the *members of the actor's own group or movement* be counted on to provide psychological, eco- nomic, or political support short of coercive force to help the actor group achieve its political objectives?

Variable 14: To what extent, in terms of their organizational cohesion and the size and geographic concentration of their resources, can *allied actor groups within the country* be counted on to provide psychological, economic, or political support short of coercive force to help the actor group achieve its political objectives?

Variable 15: To what extent, in terms of their organizational cohesion and the size and geographic proximity of their resources, can *allied groups or powers outside the country,* be counted on to provide psychological, economic, or political support short of coercive force to help the actor group achieve its political objectives?

on the subcomponents being evaluated. For example, in judging the degree of relative deprivation felt by members of a particular group for each of three subcomponents of RD, the analyst had to make subjective inferences based on past reports of overt reactions by the group's members to food shortages, lack of educational or job opportunities, repression

of political rights, etc. Similarly, estimates of an actor's perceived justification for engaging in politically violent acts, or
of the extent of coercive force or institutional support available to him, had to be inferred in most cases from reports of
statements or behavior of actor groups and allied groups,
rather than from hard evidence bearing directly on the variable in question. If the analyst was uncertain, either because
he didn't have sufficient information on an actor, or because
he found it difficult to conceive of a relationship between a
certain variable and an actor, he was expected to make an
"educated guess" at the right score, based on his subjective
impressions of the general political situation. The assumption
here was that even a "hunch" judgment by an expert on the
country under observation was likely to have some factual
basis. It would thus presumably fall within a limited range
around a "true" valuation and distort reality less than if the
expert had left the scoring box blank.

After completing the Figure 3 worksheet, the analyst
used a similar worksheet to assess each actor in terms of the
fourfold classification of proregime and antiregime and elite-
mass characteristics shown in Figure 2. That is, he had to
decide what proportion of each actor (conceived as a national
grouping) could be described as proregime and what proportion as antiregime (the two proportions had to total 10).
Then he had to determine the degree to which the actor
group was mass-oriented or elite-oriented (again the two proportions had to total 10). As in the evaluation of variables,
the analyst was expected to allocate proportions to each
actor category, based on general impressions inferred from
available information rather than on precise knowledge of
attitudes and orientations of the actor.

After he completed the two worksheets, the analyst's
scores on each subcomponent in the model were apportioned
in terms of the four actor-orientation scores he assigned each

actor. That is, the analyst's score on each subcomponent for each actor on the Figure 3 worksheet was broken down and reassigned to specific actor categories according to the way the analyst assessed that actor's proregime and antiregime attitude and mass-elite orientation. To do this, the analyst's two sets of 0-10 scores representing proportions of proregime, antiregime and mass-elite characteristics for each actor were transformed by simple cross-multiplication into four percentages totalling 100. Each percentage represented the analyst's assessment of the extent to which that actor possessed each of the four combined actor orientations— proregime mass-oriented (PR-MO), proregime elite-oriented (PR-EO), antiregime mass-oriented (AR-MO), and antiregime elite-oriented (AR-EO). The analyst's score for that actor on each subcomponent on the Figure 3 worksheet was then divided into four parts corresponding to the four percentages. If an actor was judged by the analyst to be 60 percent PR-MO, 20 percent PR-EO, and 20 percent AR-EO, the analyst's score on each subcomponent for that actor was allocated in the same proportion among those three actor categories. The same procedure was followed for all actors selected as politically significant in the country under examination.

The four resulting sets of scores for each analyst were thus divided among four subworksheets of the Figure 3 worksheet, one for each actor category. The number in each subcomponent box on each of the four subworksheets represented precisely that portion of the analyst's initial score which corresponded to the PR-MO, PR-EO, AR-MO, and AR-EO orientations he, in effect, assigned to each actor. The scores were averaged along each horizontal line on each of the four Figure 3 subworksheets to produce a mean score for each of the 11 subcomponents. In a five-member panel of country analysts, this produced 20 (5 x 4) sets of 11 subcomponent scores—one for each of the five analysts for each of

the four actor categories. These mean scores, when transposed onto a summary data sheet (see Figure 5 in which data
from the Chilean test—described in Section IV—are displayed), became the basis for projecting the causal relationships posited by the model.

In the next level of aggregation, values for key variables
(variable number 4, 7, 8, 12, 16, 17, and 18) were calculated,
based on the panel's averaged scores in each actor category.
These calculations reflected the linear relationships posited
by the Gurr theory. That is, as can be seen in the Figure 5
summary data sheet, units of value assigned by the analyst in
his evaluations were assumed to be equivalent and comparable among the model's variables, and thus to have equal, uni-
directional, and additive effects on the model's final dependent variable, the potential for political violence.

An exception to this assumption was made in the relationship between RD and justification for violence. In this case,
it was assumed that a multiplicative rather than an additive
relationship more accurately reflected reality. First, multiplication gives greater weight to RD compared to the societal
variables of coercive force and institutional support, and thus
makes the model reflect more accurately the Gurr theory's
emphasis on RD as the principal motivating force in the
causal chain leading to political violence. Secondly, multiplication better expresses what appears to be a mutually reinforcing, or mutually dampening, relationship between RD
and justification. That is, to illustrate the reinforcing function, as men become more frustrated in attempts to reduce
the discrepancy between their expectations and achievements, they are more likely to find reasons for venting their
frustration in aggression against political targets which seem
to them to be the frustrating agents. Conversely, to the
extent they become convinced that such aggression is "right"
and has a chance to succeed, the very process of thus rational-

izing their efforts will tend to reinforce their collective discontent as a motivating force toward political violence. On the dampening side, as the gap between expectations and achievements narrows, frustration diminishes and men are less likely to seek grounds for aggression. Conversely, as their basis for believing aggression is either right or practical weakens, their sense of frustration is likely to be less deeply grounded as a propelling force for aggression. In either case, assuming either a reciprocally reinforcing or a dampening effect, multiplication rather than addition appears to be the more accurate mathematical expression of the actual relationship between RD and justification. Thus, panel members' averaged scores, as transposed on the Figure 5 summary data sheet, were combined in the following ways to produce scores in each vertical column for key variables in the model:

Among the social and psychological variables, each analyst's RD scores (lines 1, 2, and 3) were added to produce a score for total RD or collective frustration (line 4). The two justification scores (lines 5 and 6) were added to produce a total justification score (line 7). This was then multiplied by the collective frustration score (line 4), to produce a score for politicized frustration (line 8).

Among the societal variables, the analyst's scores for types of coercive force (lines 9, 10, and 11) were added to produce a score for total available coercive force (line 12). Similarly, scores for types of institutional support (lines 13, 14, and 15) were added to produce a score for total available institutional support (line 16). This, added to total coercive force (line 12), produced a score for total capability for political violence (line 17).

The potential for political violence (line 18), the total of all psychological and societal variables in the model, was calculated as the sum of politicized frustration (line 8) and total capability for political violence (line 17).

Figure 5

Analyst Scores for Variables and Subcomponents, Arranged According to Actor Category (data from Chilean test)

VARIABLES	VARIABLE NUMBER	PROREGIME MASS-ORIENTED (PR-MO) Analysts A	B	C	D	E	Md.	PROREGIME ELITE-ORIENTED (PR-EO) Analysts A	B	C	D	E	Md.
Social and Psychological Variables													
A. Actor's perception of RD re:													
1. Economic conditions	1	2.21	1.69	1.28	.82	1.34	1.34	.73	.49	1.18	.79	.90	.79
2. Self improvement and social status	2	2.18	1.42	1.12	.72	.70	1.12	.74	.32	1.51	.74	.68	.74
3. Political participation	3	2.20	1.77	1.33	.72	.61	1.33	.72	.52	1.45	.84	.87	.84
Total RD or collective frustration (Sum of variables 1, 2, 3)	4	6.59	4.88	3.73	2.26	2.65	3.79	2.19	1.33	4.14	2.37	2.45	2.37
B. Actor's belief that, to reduce RD, violence is justified:													
1. On normative grounds	5	1.88	1.89	1.09	.84	.82	1.09	.58	.41	1.18	.77	.60	.60
2. On utilitarian grounds	6	1.82	1.98	1.16	.79	1.00	1.16	.59	.43	1.41	.68	.83	.68
Total justification (Sum of variables 5 & 6)	7	3.70	3.87	2.25	1.63	1.82	2.25	1.17	.84	2.59	1.45	1.43	1.28
Total politicized frustration (Product of variables 4 & 7)	8	24.38	18.89	8.39	3.68	4.82	8.53	2.56	1.12	10.72	3.32	3.51	3.03
Societal Variables													
C. Coercive force available to Actor													
1. Within own group	9	1.74	2.20	1.06	.61	.70	1.06	.41	.48	1.10	.43	.54	.48
2. From other actors	10	1.77	2.55	.93	.83	1.19	1.19	.49	.55	1.06	.61	.46	.55
3. From external allies	11	.97	1.64	.51	.33	.31	.51	.33	.48	.57	.24	.23	.33
Total available coercive force (Sum of variables 9, 10, 11)	12	4.48	6.39	2.50	1.77	2.20	2.76	1.23	1.51	2.73	1.28	1.23	1.36
D. Institutional support available													
1. Within own group	13	1.98	2.01	1.29	.68	.90	1.29	.58	.68	1.57	.47	.73	.68
2. From other actors	14	1.75	2.29	.95	.79	.98	.98	.52	.68	1.12	.63	.47	.63
3. From external allies	15	.84	1.58	.79	.34	.59	.79	.29	.58	1.00	.27	.25	.29
Total available institutional support (Sum of variables 13, 14, 15)	16	4.57	5.88	3.03	1.81	2.47	3.06	1.39	1.94	3.69	1.37	1.45	1.60
Total capability for political violence (Sum of variables 12 & 16)	17	9.05	12.27	5.53	3.58	4.67	5.82	2.62	3.45	6.42	2.65	2.68	2.96
Potential for political violence (Sum of variables 8 & 17)	18	33.43	31.16	13.92	7.26	9.49	14.35	5.18	4.57	17.14	5.97	6.19	5.99

Totals in vertical columns may not in all cases agree with those in horizontal columns because of round-off problems.
All figures are consistent with vertical column calculations.

Figure 5 Continued

VARIABLE NUMBER	ANTIREGIME MASS-ORIENTED (AR-MO) Analysts						ANTIREGIME ELITE-ORIENTED (AR-EO) Analysts						ALL ACTORS Sum of Median Analyst Scores
	A	B	C	D	E	Md.	A	B	C	D	E	Md.	
1	2.23	1.60	.83	1.66	1.28	1.60	2.00	2.03	1.52	3.05	2.67	2.03	5.76
2	2.06	1.09	.83	1.43	.76	1.09	2.02	1.16	2.48	2.66	1.73	2.02	4.97
3	1.90	1.61	.88	1.40	.91	1.40	1.95	2.07	2.72	3.05	2.48	2.48	6.05
4	6.19	4.30	2.54	4.49	2.95	4.09	5.97	5.26	6.72	8.76	6.88	6.53	16.78
5	1.63	1.53	.64	1.14	.71	1.14	1.24	1.43	2.22	2.21	1.26	1.43	4.26
6	1.65	1.55	.77	1.07	1.03	1.07	1.36	1.59	2.69	2.05	2.40	2.05	4.96
7	3.28	3.08	1.41	2.21	1.74	2.21	2.60	3.02	4.91	4.26	3.66	3.48	9.22
8	20.30	13.24	3.58	9.92	5.14	9.04	15.52	15.89	33.00	37.32	25.18	22.72	43.32*
9	2.00	1.77	.70	.97	.68	.97	1.34	1.85	2.10	1.96	1.27	1.85	4.36
10	1.95	2.06	.75	1.30	.82	1.30	1.24	2.12	2.46	2.52	1.33	2.12	5.16
11	.81	1.35	.37	.41	.18	.41	.80	1.76	1.35	.95	.44	.95	2.20
12	4.76	5.18	1.82	2.68	1.68	2.68	3.38	5.73	5.91	5.43	3.04	4.92	11.72
13	1.87	1.73	.91	.98	.86	.98	1.44	2.28	2.77	1.41	2.50	2.28	5.23
14	1.53	1.94	.79	1.13	.73	1.13	1.23	2.34	2.40	1.94	1.56	1.94	4.68
15	.76	1.31	.65	.42	.23	.65	.75	2.02	1.88	.88	.48	.88	2.61
16	4.16	4.98	2.35	2.53	1.82	2.76	3.42	6.64	7.05	4.23	4.54	5.10	12.52
17	8.92	10.16	4.17	5.21	3.50	5.44	6.80	12.37	12.96	9.66	7.58	10.02	24.24
18	29.22	23.40	7.75	15.13	8.64	14.48	22.32	28.26	45.96	46.98	32.76	32.74	67.56

* Sum of variable 8 scores across all actor categories.

Within each actor category in the Figure 5 data sheet, the median of the five analysts' scores was taken as the measure of central tendency.[2] These median scores, displayed in the final "Md." column within each actor category and in the extreme right-hand column for "all actors" thus became indicators of the comparative strength of each variable for each type of actor and hence measures of the determinants, capabilities, and potential for political violence in the country under observation.

Projecting the Types of Violence

The model's projections of the forms political violence might assume in a given country—turmoil, insurgency, conspiracy, or internal war—are based on Gurr's theoretical propositions, expanded in some cases by logical inference or from the present author's own observations and experience. Listed below are the hypothesized conditions for each type of violence and the expected relationships between actors which correspond to those conditions. Variable numbers cited in parentheses refer to scores in relevant actor-category "median" (Md.) columns of the Figure 5 data sheet. Following the list is a description of the statistical method used to determine the extent to which analyst scoring patterns meet the hypothesized conditions for the four types of political violence.

Turmoil

(1) Total RD or Collective Frustration. *Hypothesis:* The likelihood of turmoil varies directly with the intensity and scope of mass relative deprivation and inversely with the intensity and scope of elite relative deprivation (Gurr, p. 335).[3] If intense discontent is found among ordinary people but not

among the elite, the potential for riots and demonstrations is high (p. 341). *Expected Relationship:* RD (variable 4) is generally high among antiregime mass actors, low among anti-regime elite actors.

(2) Justification. *Hypothesis:* Diverse ideologies, slogans, and rumors can mobilize people for political violence. They are most likely to do so if people are intensely discontented (p. 197). If expectancy of violence is great, the intensity and scope of normative jusifications for political violence vary strongly with the intensity and scope of RD (p. 363). If members of a community see similar groups elsewhere making gains through political violence, they are likely to see utilitarian justifications for violent tactics for themselves (p. 231). In short, justifications for violence vary directly with intensity of discontent and expectancy of violence within an actor group and with the success, if any, of other groups' use of violence. *Expected Relationship:* The belief that violence is justified to reduce RD (variable 7) is stronger among antiregime mass actors than among antiregime elite actors (per turmoil hypothesis 1).

(3) Coercive Force. *Hypothesis:* Turmoil is more likely to occur when dissidents are weak relative to the regime (p. 235). Chronic turmoil is most likely when the balance of co-ercive control markedly favors the regime (p. 236). Whatever the incidence of RD, the likelihood of turmoil is high if the regime has high coercive capacities vis-à-vis the politically dis-contented (p. 341). *Expected Relationship:* Coercive force (variable 12) available to antiregime mass actors is relatively low; coercive force available to proregime elite actors is rela-tively high.

(4) Institutional Support. *Hypothesis:* Turmoil is charac-terized by diffuseness and lack of organization (p. 335). Whatever the incidence of RD, the likelihood of turmoil is high if the politically discontented are poorly organized

(p. 341). The likelihood of turmoil thus varies inversely with the degree and scope of institutional support available to mass actors. *Expected Relationship:* Institutional support (variable 16) available to antiregime mass actors is relatively low; institutional support available to proregime elite actors is relatively high.

Insurgency

(1) Total RD or Collective Frustration. *Hypothesis:* The likelihood of conspiracy (defined by Gurr to include both insurgency and attempted coups) varies directly with the intensity and scope of elite relative deprivation and inversely with the intenstiy and scope of mass relative deprivation (p. 335). *Expected Relationship:* RD (variable 4) is generally high among antiregime elite actors, low among antiregime mass actors.

(2) Justification. *Hypothesis:* Justifications for violence vary directly with the intensity of discontent and expectancy of violence within an actor group and with the success, if any, of other groups' use of violence. (See turmoil hypothesis 2). *Expected Relationship:* The belief that violence is justified to reduce RD (variable 7) is stronger among antiregime elite actors than among antiregime mass actors (per insurgency hypothesis 1).

(3) Coercive Force. *Hypothesis:* Conspirators are likely to resort to clandestine operations if the regime makes repressive rather than adjustive responses to demands made through conventional channels or by public protest (p. 236). Inflexible, repressive responses intensify the hostility of the conspirators and reduce their hopes of obtaining reform except through revolutionary transformation (p. 236). The result is to turn conspirators toward active terrorist or guerrilla operations. *Expected Relationship:* Coercive force

(variable 12) available to antiregime elite actors is relatively low; coercive force available to proregime elite actors is relatively high.

(4) Institutional Support. *Hypothesis:* Conspirators who resort to clandestine operations against the regime may, if they find that regime forces remain unshakably loyal to the ruling elite, resort to terrorism or small-scale guerrilla warfare with the objective of eroding regime strength over the long run and of increasing popular discontent (p. 343). To the degree conspirators find themselves thwarted by strong, institutional proregime forces, they are likely to turn to insurgency. *Expected Relationship:* Institutional support (variable 16) available to antiregime elite actors is relatively low; institutional support available to proregime actors is relatively high.

Conspiracy

(1) Total RD or Collective Frustration. *Hypothesis:* (same as insurgency hypothesis 1 above). The likelihood of conspiracy (defined by Gurr to include both insurgency and attempted coups) varies directly with the intensity and scope of elite relative deprivation and inversely with the intensity and scope of mass relative deprivation (p. 335). *Expected Relationship:* RD (variable 4) is generally high among antiregime elite actors, low among antiregime mass actors.

(2) Justification. *Hypothesis:* A coup attempt is most likely when its leaders estimate that regime incumbents can compel neither military nor popular support and that they can consequently force the incumbents out of office, often with only minimal use of force (p. 236). In such circumstances, mass dissidents are not as strongly frustrated as elite coup-plotters (see conspiracy hypothesis 1 above), and have relatively little reason to justify violence against the regime.

Elite conspirators, on the other hand, though highly discontented, believe that regime incumbents can be removed in a quick "bloodless" action and thus also tend to discount the desirability of violence. *Expected Relationship:* The belief that violence is justified to reduce RD (variable 7) is relatively low for both antiregime elite and antiregime mass actors.

(3) Coercive Force. *Hypothesis:* If dissidents have, or think they have, a high ratio of coercive control relative to the regime, they are likely to resort to conspiracy: there is no need to organize an internal war when power can be seized in a precise thrust at a weakened regime. This is the classic pattern of the successful coup d'état (p. 236). *Expected Relationship:* Coercive force (variable 12) available to antiregime elite actors is relatively high; coercive force available to proregime elite actors is relatively low.

(4) Institutional Support. *Hypothesis:* Coups d'état typically occur and political concessions are most readily granted by elites under threat of violence when the balance of social control and support favors the dissidents (p. 321). Conspiratorial activities are best prosecuted if dissatisfied elites can develop tight-knit organizations (p. 341). *Expected Relationship:* Institutional support (variable 16) available to antiregime elite actors is relatively high; institutional support available to proregime elite actors is relatively low.

Internal War

(1) Total RD or Collective Frustration. *Hypothesis:* The likelihood of internal war varies directly with the intensity and scope of elite and mass relative deprivation (p. 336). Mass revolutionary and secessionist movements are most likely to develop if discontent is widespread and intense among both elite and mass (p. 343). *Expected Relationship:* RD (variable 4) is relatively high among antiregime elite and mass

actors, relatively low among proregime elite and mass actors.

(2) Justification. *Hypothesis:* Justifications for violence vary directly with intensity of discontent and expectancy of violence within an actor group and with the success, if any, of other groups' use of violence (see turmoil hypothesis 2). *Expected Relationship:* The belief that violence is justified to reduce RD (variable 7) is relatively high for both antiregime elite and antiregime mass actors (per internal war hypothesis 1).

(3) Coercive Force. *Hypothesis:* The more closely the coercive capacities of dissidents approach those of the regime, the more protracted and intense political violence is likely to be (p. 343). *Expected Relationship:* Coercive force (variable 12) available to proregime and antiregime actors is uniformly high.

(4) Institutional Support. *Hypothesis:* Turmoil is characterized by diffuseness and lack of organization, internal war by their opposites (p. 335). The more closely the institutional capacities of dissidents approach those of the regime, the more protracted and intense political violence is likely to be (p. 343). *Expected Relationship:* Institutional support (variable 16) available to proregime and antiregime actors is uniformly high.

Calculating the Scoring Patterns

The median scores of the five-member panel of analysts in the initial Chilean test (described in the following section) for each actor category in the above hypothesized relationships are shown in Figure 6. The median scores are in the column immediately to the right of the "Type of Actor" column. Projected high (H) and low (L) designations derived from each of the above hypothesized scoring patterns are indicated in the vertical column for each type of violence.

Figure 6

Median Analyst Scores Applied to Four Conditions Hypothesized for Each Type of Political Violence (data from Chilean test)

CONDI-TION	VARIABLE	No.	TYPE OF ACTOR	ANALYSTS MEDIAN SCORES	TURMOIL Required Pattern	TURMOIL Ratio	INSURGENCY Required Pattern	INSURGENCY Ratio	CONSPIRACY Required Pattern	CONSPIRACY Ratio	INTERNAL WAR Required Pattern	INTERNAL WAR Ratio
A	Total RD or collective frustration	4	PR-MO	3.79							L	
			PR-EO	2.37							L	
			AR-MO	4.09	H	.63	L	1.60	L	1.60	H	1.72
			AR-EO	6.53	L		H		H		H	
					X		X		X		X	
B	Total justification for violence	7	PR-MO	2.25					H		L	
			PR-EO	1.25					H		L	
			AR-MO	2.21	H	.64	L	1.57	L	.62	H	1.61
			AR-EO	3.48	L		H		L		H	
					+		+		+		+	
C	Total available coercive force	12	PR-MO	2.76							H	
			PR-EO	1.36	H	.51	H		L		H	
			AR-MO	2.68	L			.28		3.62	H	.54
			AR-EO	4.92			L		H		H	
					+		+		+		+	
D	Total available institutional support	16	PR-MO	3.06							H	
			PR-EO	1.06	H	.58	H		L		H	
			AR-MO	2.76	L			.31		3.19	H	.59
			AR-EO	5.10			L		H		H	
					=		=		=		=	
	Ratio Totals				1.49		3.10		7.80		3.89	

PR-MO=Proregime, mass-oriented actors
PR-EO=Proregime, elite-oriented actors
AR-MO=Antiregime, mass-oriented actors
AR-EO=Antiregime, elite-oriented actors

Note: Letter designations indicate high (H) and low (L) levels of strength of those variables hypothesized as necessary to produce fulfillment of the conditions for each type of violence. Numbers following the letter designations are ratios between median scores for relevant actor categories for each condition. Ratio totals are calculated by combining the four ratios in each "Type-of-violence" column in the same manner as that used to determine the model's main dependent variable potential for political violence (PPV), i.e., PPV=(RD ·Justification) · Coercive Force · Institutional Support.

The test of fulfillment or nonfulfillment of the hypothesized condition is whether or not the median scores conform to the indicated H and L designations. For example, the first of the four scoring patterns under Condition A for turmoil (derived from Hypothesis 1 above for turmoil) is an H score for AR-MO and an L score for AR-EO on Variable 4 (total RD or collective frustration). The actual median scores assigned by the panel in this case failed to conform to the required pattern: the score of 4.09 for AR-MO is clearly low, not high, relative to the score of 6.53 for AR-EO. On the other hand, those same scores for AR-MO and AR-EO do fulfill the adjacent reverse L-H relationship hypothesized as Condition A for insurgency (derived from Hypothesis 1 above for insurgency). In this case, the scores of 4.09 for AR-MO and 6.53 for AR-EO clearly conform to the required pattern.

In the Figure 6 table, the panel's median scores in the Chilean test for the sixteen hypothesized relationships—eleven H-L or L-H relationships involving only two actor categories and five HH-LL, LL-HH, or HHHH relationships involving all four actor categories—were transformed into ratios representing the degree of fulfillment or nonfulfillment of the requisite conditions for each type of violence. These ratios are recorded to the right of each hypothesized relationship. A ratio above 1.00 indicates fulfillment of the hypothesized condition, a ratio below 1.00 indicates nonfulfillment. The degree of fulfillment or nonfulfillment is measured by the extent to which the ratio is above or below 1.00.

The ratios were calculated in the following manner: In the case of H-L or L-H relationships involving only two actor categories (all four conditions for turmoil and insurgency, and Conditions A, C, and D for conspiracy), the ratio was produced by dividing the score assigned to the actor category on the H line by that assigned to the actor category on the L line. In the case of HH-LL or LL-HH relationships involving all four actor categories (Condition B for conspiracy and Conditions A and B for internal war), the ratio was produced by dividing the average of the two scores assigned to actor categories on the two H lines by the average of the two scores assigned to actor categories on the two L lines. In the case of the two HHHH relationships required for Conditions C and D for internal war, the measure of agreement or disagreement was based on the difference between the average score of the two proregime actor categories and that of the two antiregime actor categories. It was arbitrarily assumed that if this difference was more than 25 percent of the higher of the two averaged scores, the condition of "uniformly high" capabilities for both proregime and antiregime actors, as required by the two hypothesized relationships, was not fulfilled. In the event of nonfulfillment, the ratio was calculated by dividing the lower averaged score by the higher averaged score, thereby producing a ratio value less than 1.00 to indicate disagreement with the hypothesized condition. Conversely, if the difference between the two averaged scores was found to be less than 25 percent of the higher of the two scores, it was assumed that the "uniformly high" condition was fulfilled. In this event, the reverse ratio, one with a value greater than 1.00, was produced by dividing the higher averaged score by the lower averaged score.

It can be seen from Figure 6 that, in the Chilean test, of the four conditions hypothesized for each type of violence, none was fulfilled for tumoil, two were fulfilled for insurgency, two for internal war, and three for conspiracy.

Assuming that the ratios in Figure 6 reflect not only fulfillment or nonfulfillment of requisite conditions for a particular form of violence, but also reflect the strength or weakness of corresponding key variables in the model, the four ratios in each "Type of Political Violence" column can be combined in the same way the corresponding variables were combined in the calculation for potential for political vio-lence—i.e., *PPV* = (*RD* x *Justification*) + *Coercive Force* + *Institutional Support*—to produce a figure that represents the *relative* potential for each type of political violence. If one further assumes a logical correspondence between the poten-tial for and the probability of an event occurring, the ratio totals at the bottom of Figure 6 could be interpreted as indi-cating the likelihood of each type of political violence de-veloping, relative to each of the other three types.

IV. Applying the Model

The Chilean Test

In the spring of 1974, a preliminary test was conducted to check the procedures devised to apply the model and to gain an initial assessment of the model's ability to project an accurate profile of political violence. The situation chosen for the test was the Chilean scene in mid-1973. Five intelli-gence analysts who had been close Washington observers of the Chilean situation in mid-1973 were asked to participate. Though the analysts were obviously aware that the Chilean situation had been resolved in a coup in September 1973, it was assumed that the information available to them on the kinds of subjects required by the model—i.e., the basic frus-trations, justification, coercive force, and institutional sup-port of the Chilean military and civilian actors who produced the coup—would not be significantly different from infor-mation at hand before the denouement. In any case, since the analysts would not know how their scores were aggregated to produce the final output of the model, they would have no way of discerning causal connections between the variables and relationships they were asked to assess and the type of political violence projected by the model. There was thus little chance that they could consciously or unconsciously "tip" their evaluations to produce the "right" outcome. To the extent the test produced a profile which appeared to "foresee" the Chilean coup of September 1973, we could therefore conclude that there was some tentative confirmation of the model's utility as a predictive tool.

The five panel members first agreed upon a list of thirty-one politically significant actor groups on the Chilean domestic scene in mid-1973. Using the guidance questions listed in Figure 4, each member made an independent evaluation on a ten-point scale of each of the model's eleven subcomponents for each of the thirty-one actors. On a similar ten-point scale the analyst then assessed each of the thirty-one actors in terms of his proregime or antiregime attitude and mass or elite orientation. When aggregated in the manner described above, these scores produced values for the model's main variables, actor categories, and types of anticipated violence.

As can be seen in Figure 5, the results of the test revealed considerable variation among the five panel members. (Questions of data reliability raised by disagreement among panel members are examined in Section V.) Nevertheless, the data for the panel as a whole reveal some rather clear profiles of types of actors and their propensities for particular types of violence on the Chilean scene in mid-1973:

- Among pro-Allende forces, the potential for violence was concentrated heavily in mass-oriented groups.
- The most politicized frustration was found among anti-Allende elite groups. A lesser and roughly equal amount of politicized frustration was found among pro-Allende mass groups and anti-Allende mass groups. The least amount was seen among pro-Allende elite groups.
- Similarly, anti-Allende elite groups were perceived as

having the greatest capability to engage in violence, mass groups of both pro-Allende and anti-Allende persuasion had intermediate capabilities, while pro-Allende elite had the least capability.

- Anti-Allende groups were seen to have far more potential for violence than pro-Allende groups.
- Among anti-Allende forces, elite groups had more potential for violence than mass groups.

As indicated in the Figure 6 table, there were also marked differences between conditions hypothesized as conducive to particular types of violence:

- Conditions favorable for turmoil (riots and demonstrations) were least apparent. Actors with a potential for this type of violence were deficient in all four of the requisite causal factors—RD, justification, coercive force, and institutional support.
- Conditions conducive to insurgency were considerably more apparent. Groups with potential for engaging in this type of violence seemed sufficiently frustrated and had enough justification to do so, but they were notably lacking in the coercive force and institutional support needed to carry out sustained terrorist or guerrilla operations.
- Conditions favorable for internal war were somewhat more apparent than those for insurgency. Actors sufficiently "polarized" to trigger large-scale revolutionary action or civil war appeared amply motivated (high RD and justification) but were hampered by a lack of resources (coercive force and institutional support) to carry out and sustain such major confrontations.
- Conditions conducive to conspiracy were much more

apparent than for any of the other types of violence. Those actors in a position to stage a coup against Allende seemed to lack a clear rationale (justification) for making the attempt, but their psychological motivation (RD) was sufficiently high, and they appeared to have much greater coercive force and institutional support available to back up their conspiratorial efforts, compared to the capability of pro-Allende forces to resist a coup attempt.

Since these findings seemed consistent with generally accepted judgments among Latin American watchers about the role and nature of key actors on the Chilean political scene in mid-1973, there seemed to be warrant for concluding that the model could be developed into a useful aid in profiling the potential for political violence in other conflict situations.

The Second Test Phase

Following up this tentative conclusion, we decided to apply the model next to three ongoing situations of domestic unrest or political conflict. In this second application, we wanted to see how the model tracked changes in political violence over time, rather than merely catch a one-time snapshot profile as in the Chilean case. We also wanted to see how the model would perform in societies of varying degrees of development and with different cultural heritages and political institutions. We thus hoped not only to detect shifting patterns in the magnitude and form of anticipated political violence within particular countries, but also to see how these patterns might vary between different types of countries. Because the types of trend data produced by the model in each country would be comparable, it was hoped that we might in this way lay the basis for discerning cross-cultural parameters for levels and types of political violence. Finally, in the second test phase we wanted to examine two important methodological questions: the reliability of the procedures used to apply the model (i.e., the consistency with which different analysts following the same procedures would produce similar results), and the validity of the model's findings (i.e., the extent to which those results corresponded to actual developments in each country).

Three countries, each confronted with domestic conflict of one sort or another and representing a different stage of development in a different geographic area, were selected for the test. The three were Argentina, Ethiopia, and Thailand. For each, a panel was selected, consisting of five analysts working on the country. Each panel agreed upon a list of politically significant actors in its country—thirty in Argentina, thirty-two in Ethiopia, twenty-five in Thailand. A list of the actors selected in each country is shown in Figure 7.

After an initial briefing on procedures, each panel was requested to assign evaluations (based on the Figure 4 guidance questions) to each of the model's eleven subcomponents and four actor categories at monthly intervals in the period November 1974 through June 1975. A total of seven consecutive assessments was thus produced by each panel. The data for key variables and types of actors, aggregated as described in section III, are displayed in Figures 8 through 11. For each of the three countries the data are keyed to the value for the potential for political violence (PPV) as determined by that country's five-member panel.

In general, the trends displayed in Figures 8 through 11 seem to reflect the actual course of events in each country:

(1) As shown in Figure 8, Ethiopia had the highest potential for political violence throughout the test period (averaging between 60 and 80). This coincides with the widespread disorder and violence in that country in the aftermath

Figure 7.

Politically Significant Actors in Argentina,
Ethiopia, and Thailand

Argentina

1. Justicialist Party
2. Radical Civic Union
3. Movement of Integration and Development
4. Popular Conservative Party
5. Popular Christian Party
6. Communist Party
7. Socialist Parties
8. Popular Federalist Alliance
9. Federal Police
10. State Secretariat for Intelligence (SIDE)
11. Army
12. Navy
13. Air Force
14. CGT/commercial-service unions
15. CGT/industrial unions
16. CGT/agricultural unions
17. Civil Service
18. General Economic Confederation (small and medium business)
19. Big business (domestic)
20. Foreign business community
21. Catholic Church
22. Revolutionary Workers Party (ERP)
23. Montoneros
24. Argentine Revolutionary Front (FAR)
25. Right-wing paramilitary groups
26. Youth/student groups
27. University/intellectual groups
28. Technical/scientific/professional groups
29. Press/media/journalists
30. National Rural Society (large landowners)

Ethiopia

1. Marxist/Leninist groups
2. Republicans/moderates
3. Reformers/radicals
4. Monarchists
5. Army airborne units

Figure 7. continued

6. Engineer corps
7. The Imperial Bodyguard/First Division
8. Second Division
9. Third Division
10. Fourth Division
11. Air Force
12. Navy
13. Officers' associations
14. Veterans' associations
15. Student groups
16. Landowners/provincial aristocracy
17. Urban businessmen
18. Peasants
19. Government workers
20. Truck/bus/taxi drivers
21. Technical/industrial workers
22. Agricultural workers
23. The CELU organization
24. The Church hierarchy
25. Muslims
26. Eritrean liberation groups
27. Somali-sponsored liberation groups
28. The Amhara groups
29. The Danakil tribe
30. Eritrean groups
31. The Tigreans
32. The Galla tribe and organization

Thailand

1. Socialist parties
2. Centrist parties
3. Rightist parties
4. Army
5. Air Force
6. Navy
7. National Police
8. Government workers
9. Urban industrial workers
10. Farmers
11. Big businessmen
12. Small businessmen
13. Chinese associations
14. Vietnamese community
15. Malay community
16. Hill tribes
17. Communist Party
18. Malay separatists
19. People for Democracy
20. Press/media
21. University student groups
22. Vocational student groups
23. Academics/intellectuals
24. Urban slum dwellers
25. Monarchy/Royalty/Nobility

Figure 8

Conditions Conducive to Particular Types of Political Violence

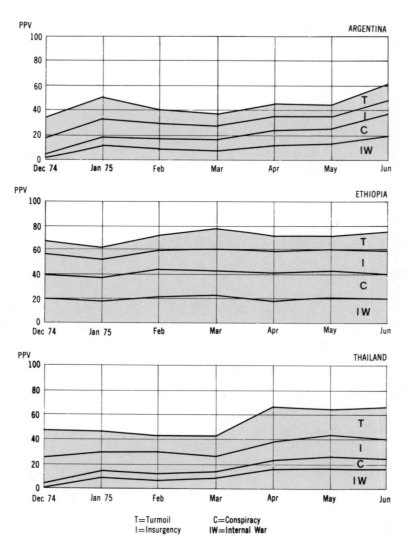

T=Turmoil   C=Conspiracy
I=Insurgency   IW=Internal War

Shaded areas represent, within the limits of each country's potential
for political violence (PPV), the degree to which that country panel's
median scores on key variables fulfill the conditions hypothesized as
conducive to each type of political violence.

of the seizure of power by the Provisional Military Action Committee (PMAC) in late 1974. As expected, through most of the period, the PPV in Argentina and Thailand ranged considerably lower (around 50). In both countries, however, the potential for violence increased markedly (up to the 60-80 range) toward the end of the test period. In Argentina, the rise occurred as Mrs. Peron's hold on power weakened and labor and military seemed to move toward confrontation. In Thailand it coincided with growing tension in the wake of continuing domestic disorder, persisting uncertainty about the prospects of the new coalition government, and the possibility of increased communist support to Thai insurgents.

(2) With some exceptions, the kinds of political violence projected by the model in Figure 8 seemed to correspond roughly to those actually prevailing in each country. In Ethiopia, the conditions conducive to conspiracy and internal war were consistently dominant. In Thailand, conditions favorable to turmoil represented the dominant trend, particularly in the April-June period. In Argentina, the pattern was less clear. Conditions conducive to insurgency—the seemingly dominant form of violence in the country—were generally deemphasized by the model, with correspondingly larger weightings given to the other three types. Also, in both Argentina and Thailand the model seemed to accord a disproportionately strong emphasis to the prospects for internal war, compared to the Ethiopian case.[4]

(3) As indicated in Figure 9, the types of actors with a propensity for political violence varied considerably during the test period, both between and within the three countries. In Argentina in December 1974, proregime Peronist groups were the strongest proponents of political violence; by June 1975, groups opposed to the Peronist government had emerged as the dominant violence-prone forces. In Ethiopia, mass and elite actors arrayed against the ruling revolutionary

Figure 9

The Potential for Political Violence (PPV) for Each Type of Actor

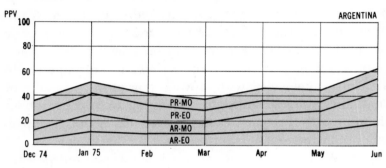

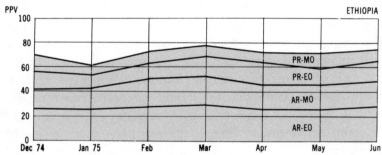

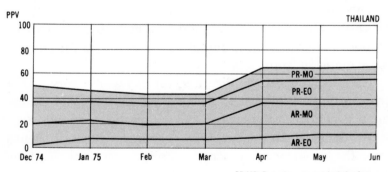

Shaded areas represent each country
panel's median scores for PPV for
each actor category.

PR-MO=Pro regime, mass-oriented actors
PR-EO =Pro regime, elite-oriented actors
AR-MO=Antiregime, mass-oriented actors
AR-MO=Anti regime, elite-oriented actors

council were consistently stronger than procouncil groups throughout the test period. In Thailand, the four types of actors were viewed as roughly equal in their potential for violence in the first half of the period; in the last half, as the new Thai coalition government began to run into difficulties, antiregime groups, particularly those which were mass-oriented, emerged as the dominant actors with a potential for violence.

(4) In Figure 10, within the changing limits of each country's potential for political violence, the pattern of actors' motivations and capabilities to engage in violence can be seen to have remained fairly stable during the test period. In all three countries, political frustration was clearly the main factor in the perceived rise and fall of PPV. On the other hand, the capability to turn that frustration into actual political violence remained relatively low, constant, and approximately equal for the three countries.[5]

Apart from the above substantive findings, the patterns of individual assessments shown in Figure 11 indicate general agreement among panel members on the major shifts in the potential for violence in each country, i.e., the gradual leveling off of PPV in Ethiopia in the latter part of the period, and the upsurge in PPV in both Argentina and Thailand in the final months of the test. But within these large bands of consensus some fairly clear deviations are apparent, i.e., the persistently low trend lines of Analysts A and B on Argentina and Analyst D on Ethiopia during much of the period, and the shorter-term deviations of Analysts B and E on Thailand. These divergencies pose interesting questions about the causes of consensus and disagreement among experts viewing the same situation. Is there a positive relationship between the range of variation and perceived uncertainty inherent in the situation under observation? To what extent do the individual deviations noted in Figure 11 reflect systematic

Figure 10

The Potential for Political Violence (PPV) for Each Type of Actor in Terms of Key Variables in the Model

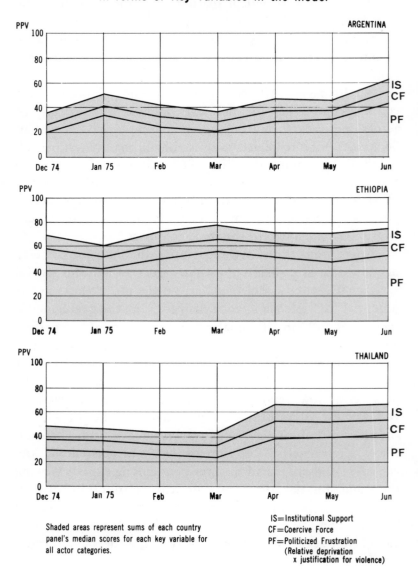

Shaded areas represent sums of each country panel's median scores for each key variable for all actor categories.

IS=Institutional Support
CF=Coercive Force
PF=Politicized Frustration
   (Relative deprivation
    x justification for violence)

Figure 11

Individual Analysts' Assessments of the Potential
for Political Violence (PPV)

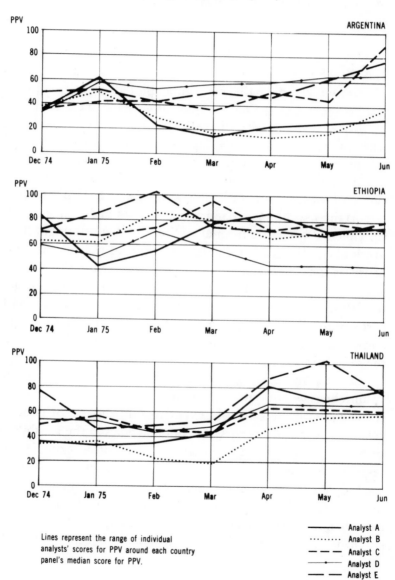

Lines represent the range of individual
analysts' scores for PPV around each country
panel's median score for PPV.

——————— Analyst A
·················· Analyst B
— — — Analyst C
—•—•— Analyst D
— — Analyst E

differences in bureaucratic vantage points? In professional backgrounds? In the amount or type of information available to the analyst? Or in the analyst's preoccupation with or proximity to the scene?[6] Such questions suggest a tantalizing agenda of hypotheses for future research.

V. Critique of the Model

Notwithstanding the many unexplored areas, our initial tests suggest that the Gurr model, as we have operationalized it, can provide tangible benefits to the analyst concerned with political conflict. During the seven-month test period the model produced useful profiles of the potential for political violence and of the conditions conducive to particular types of violence in the countries examined. It pinpointed important psychological and social factors underlying political violence which traditional methods of analysis might have overlooked. It made available a measure of the relative propensities for violence among various groups in the three countries. Finally, as an important by-product, it provided a potentially useful means for monitoring the extent of, and perhaps for gaining a better understanding of, the causes of consensus and disagreement among experts concerned with the same conflict situation.

Serious methodological problems remain, however. A comprehensive critique of the model by a team of academic researchers with considerable experience in the use of expert-generated data points to serious deficiencies in the reliability of the model's data and the validity of its projections.[7] With respect to reliability, the critique, as anticipated, found general agreement among panel members on the major shifts in the potential for violence in each country. But within these large bands of consensus, as we have seen, there were consistently wide differences of judgment between individual panel members. In general, the level of data reliability was consistently low across country, across waves of assessments, and across major actor groupings. On the other hand, some variables in the model, e.g., relative deprivation (RD), seemed to yield more reliable judgments than others. Moreover, the reliability of assessments seemed to vary with differing perceived conditions in each country. In particular, disagreement among panel members appeared to vary directly with the perceived level of violence in the country, i.e., increases in violence seemed to deepen analyst uncertainty about the meaning and dimensions of the violence and thus led to increased disagreement among panel members. Finally, rather clear differences in evaluative judgments were found to be related to the differing professional and bureaucratic perspectives of the individual analysts. Thus, the data produced by the model appeared subject to a degree of variation that was a function both of procedural problems in the model itself and of the differing perceptions and information available on the country under observation.

To test the validity of the model's ability to produce an accurate profile of political violence and to predict the magnitude and form of violence in the three countries, independent measures of actual political violence derived from daily FBIS reports and from daily issues of a current intelligence publication were correlated with the model's PPV scores for each month during the test period. In addition, in an attempt to test in greater detail the validity of the model's output in a single country, a data set based on all reports of political violence in Argentina from a variety of sources was compared with the model's monthly PPV values for that country during the test period.

These tests failed to produce clear correlational patterns between independently measured political violence and the model's projections. They provided little on which to base firm conclusions about the model's ability to profile and predict political violence. The patterns which emerged suggested that the model in its present form can serve as a barometer of violence, but only in a very gross and insensitive way. It seems able to predict large changes in political violence, i.e., when the violence exceeds a certain threshold and becomes extraordinary in reference to an established norm. Within this range of normality, however, it was unable to anticipate smaller fluctuations in either the level or form of violence.

In short, the model seems to provide a valid means of profiling the *basic* determinants of political violence. Also, it appears to have some capability to anticipate major changes in that profile over time. In some cases, it can illuminate conditions conducive to certain types of violence. As to the model's predictive capability, however, the results of our tests must be regarded at this stage as ambiguous and inconclusive.

VI. Suggested Modifications in Future Applications

Our critique suggests several ways in which the model's present deficiencies might be remedied or at least minimized. Reliability could be improved by reducing the number of variables, using a smaller scale to evaluate subcomponents, and defining terms more precisely. Reliability would also be improved, and the utility of the model enhanced, if data on actors and variables were aggregated at the analyst level and keyed to actors and areas of special interest to the analyst, and if judgmental differences on specific variables and actions were displayed to illuminate areas of consensus and disagreement among different analysts and Agency components. Finally, the accuracy of the model's projections could be sharpened by calculating different weightings for key variables in each country and by introducing environmental factors, like stability of political institutions and historical patterns of violence, which determine the significance of changes in levels of conflict in particular countries. One way to fine-tune and expand the model along these lines would be to develop a system dynamics version, in which one could build in assumptions and data derived from ongoing observations of the nature and course of political violence in the country under observation.

In conjunction with the above modifications, it would be useful to develop and maintain an independent measure of political violence for each country or situation to which the model might be applied. This separate measure could be a simple frequency count of violent events, keyed to the same time intervals employed by the model and coded according to indicators of particular forms of violence from a regular intelligence product. The measure would serve several purposes. It could be used as an independent data base at the analyst level against which to assess the accuracy of the model's output. It could be used to tailor the model's variables by mutliple regression to a particular country situation. And it could be monitored independently of the model to test the hypothesis that—on the assumption that the past and present contain the seeds of tomorrow's changes —current trends in political violence can be used to predict the nature and magnitude of coming violence in a country.

Taken together, these modifications would aim, on the one hand, at simplifying the model and tailoring it more closely to anlayst needs and, on the other, at expanding the model's scope to include additional explanatory factors and alternative methods of analysis. The suggested changes could be introduced piecemeal in successive applications of the model to new ongoing situations of conflict. To minimize confusion and the burden on participating analysts, however, it might be preferable to do as much of the remodeling as possible before reapplying the model at the working level.

Notes

1. A systematic elaboration of the theory is presented in Ted Robert Gurr, *Why Men Rebel* (Princeton, New Jersey: Princeton University Press, 1970).

2. The median, rather than mean, was used to minimize distortion which might result from extreme or "outlying" evaluations of a single expert on a small five-member panel.

3. Page references in this and subsequent hypotheses are to Gurr's *Why Men Rebel.* Hypothetical statements without page references are the present author's extrapolations or inferences from Gurr's statements.

4. One could speculate, on the other hand, that, in the Argentine case at least, the relatively sharp rise in conditions for internal war in the final month of the test period reflected a very real and apparently growing sense of political polarization in the country, even though the dimensions of political violence projected by the model did not appear to have reached the "internal war" stage. In this sense, to the extent the model has validity as a predictor, it may be anticipating the precursory political and social conditions conducive to a particular type of violence as well as the manifestation of the violence itself.

5. The consistently high strength and volatility of politicized frustration was to be expected, of course, because of the relatively greater weight given in the theoretical design of the model to RD and justification—the motivating variables behind politicized frustration—compared to coercive force and institutional support—the factors which constitute capability. Within the large ranges of politicized frustration generated by the model, however, significant differences are evident in the way politicized frustration fluctuated in the three countries.

6. On the latter point, the case of Analyst E on the Thai panel is especially interesting. E's period of deviation coincided almost exactly with his temporary residence in Thailand from January through March 1975. During this three-month period, while his normal working contacts with other members of the panel were interrupted, and he was viewing developments in the country first hand, his trend line, based on

regular monthly assessments relayed from Thailand, showed a marked decline in his estimate of PPV in the country. Upon his return, however, his trend line moved steadily back into a higher and relatively narrow band of consensus with his colleagues.

7. The critique was prepared by Professors William D. Coplin and Michael K. O'Leary and their research assistants, Rodger M. Govea and Donald J. McMaster, at Syracuse University. Descriptions and results of statistical tests, and specific recommendations drawn from the critique, are contained in the full report available from the Library of Congress.

6

Content Analysis: Measuring Support for Brezhnev

Richards J. Heuer, Jr.

The degree of support for, and potential opposition to, the top man within the Soviet leadership is a topic of continuing interest to analysts of Soviet political dynamics. Inferences concerning where a given Soviet leader stands vis-à-vis the Party chief are usually based on some combination of four kinds of evidence: the career pattern of the leader or his close associates, his known policy positions, his appearance or ranking on various protocol occasions, and the references he makes to the top figure in public speeches or writings.

This study analyzes the fourth type of evidence with respect to references to General Secretary Leonid I. Brezhnev made in the first three months of 1976 by sixteen major regional political leaders, seven of whom are also members of the Politburo. The primary objective is to test empirically the validity and reliability of four indicators that are, or might be, used by Kremlinologists to judge the nature of a leader's attitude toward the general secretary of the Communist Party of the Soviet Union (CPSU). The sixteen leaders are compared on the basis of their political support and personal relationship with Brezhnev, as determined through quantitative content analysis of these indicators in three sets of speeches given shortly before, during, and just after the Twenty-fifth CPSU Party Congress. The results of the content analysis are then compared with independent judgments about the sixteen Soviet leaders made by a panel of three CIA analysts, each expert in internal Soviet political affairs. To the extent that the content analysis results and expert opinion conform, there is support for the validity of the indicators.

The Twenty-fifth CPSU Party Congress, held in Moscow from 24 February to 5 March 1976, was preceded by a series of congresses at subordinate echelons of the Party hierarchy and followed by reports on the main congress to regional and local Party *aktivs*.[1] Thus the key regional Party leaders made three major speeches in a short span of time: to their republic or equivalent Party congress during January or February 1976, to the Twenty-fifth Party Congress in Moscow, and to a meeting of their republic or equivalent Party *aktiv* during March 1976. The complete text is available for the first two sets of speeches, and very lengthy extracts are available on the third.[2]

These three sets of speeches provide a particularly rich source of data for comparing the public positions taken by different Soviet leaders. Because all sixteen leaders spoke at more or less the same time, for the same general purpose, and to the same or similar audiences, we have the best possible basis that one can reasonably expect to find for comparing the different leaders' speeches to one another. Since each regional leader made three successive speeches, we can also gain some impression of his consistency in expressing particular positions. One may reasonably conclude that public differences consistently expressed in these speeches reflect actual differences in the personal viewpoints or self-perceived interests of the speakers.[3]

To cross-check conclusions about the indicators drawn

from this one time period, the data base was extended in time to include speeches from the Twenty-fourth and Twenty-second Party Congresses by the same leaders or their predecessors in the same regional leadership positions. The Twenty-fourth Party Congress (1971) was another Brezhnev congress, but one at which references to him were far less frequent than at the Twenty-fifth Party Congress. The Twenty-second Party Congress, held in 1961 at the height of Khrushchev's power, was selected because the high frequency of laudatory references to Khrushchev makes it somewhat comparable to the Twenty-fifth Party Congress.

The leaders were selected for inclusion in the analysis on the basis of their political importance and the availability of a series of related and comparable speeches. These leaders are the Party first secretaries of fourteen republics (excluding the RSFSR, which does not have its own party organization) and the Leningrad Oblast and Moscow City Party organizations. Seven of the current first secretaries are also full or candidate members of the Politburo. The sixteen current leaders are: V. V. Grishin, Moscow City, full member; D. A. Kunayev, Kazakhstan, full member; G. V. Romanov, Leningrad Oblast, full member; V. V. Shcherbitsky, Ukraine, full member; G. A. Aliyev, Azerbaydzhan, candidate member; P. M. Masherov, Belorussia, candidate member; Sh. R. Rashidov, Uzbekistan, candidate member; I. I. Bodyul, Moldavia; K. S. Demirchyan, Armenia; M. G. Gapurov, Turkmenistan; P. Grishkyavichus, Lithuania; I. G. Kebin, Estonia; D. R. Rasulov, Tadzhikistan; E. A. Shevardnadze, Georgia; T. U. Usubaliyev, Kirgiz; and E. E. Voss, Latvia.

The Twenty-fifth Party Congress was characterized by various signs of enhanced personal prestige for Brezhnev. All speakers expressed "full" support for his leadership. The Soviet system, after all, places a premium on an outward appearance of Party harmony and unanimity. But divergent

views do exist, and they are expressed publicly even during
such ritualistic performances as a Party congress.

> Since partisan statements on contentious subjects cannot be
> made explicitly, they take the form of esoteric communi-
> cations—texts whose deepest meanings can be grasped by only
> a part of their audience. . . . The vehicles for these veiled
> messages are the standard formulas and stereotyped phrases
> out of which authoritative Soviet speeches and articles are con-
> structed. Seemingly trivial changes in this ritualisitic language
> produce messages for interested subelites.[4]

By using a systematic procedure to note and compare all
references to Brezhnev, this study seeks to identify and
interpret certain of these esoteric communications.

Prior to analysis of the data, a panel of three analysts
specializing in Soviet internal politics, one analyst from
each of three different offices of the Agency, was con-
vened to discuss potential indicators of support for Brezhnev.
Nine potential indicators were identified, and the analysts
were asked to comment on whether each one could be
expected to yield a valid measure of support for Brezhnev.
This discussion generated a series of hypotheses to be
checked against the empirical data, but the ensuing analysis
was conducted in an exploratory mode rather than as explicit
hypothesis testing. This report covers only four of the nine
potential indicators. These four indicators and their operational definitions are as follows.[5]

"Leonid Il'ich." All references to Brezhnev by his
first name and patronymic are counted, and inferences
are drawn from the frequency with which a leader uses this
informal mode of address. Frequencies for the three speeches
combined ranged from Aliyev's seven references to Leonid
Il'ich to no such references at all by Romanov, Usubaliyev,
Voss, Kebin, and Masherov.

"Omitting 'Comrade.'" This refers to omission of "Comrade" when referring to the Soviet leader by his last name, e.g., reference to Leonid Il'ich Brezhnev rather than Comrade Leonid Il'ich Brezhnev. In scoring this indicator, the number of omissions is expressed as a percentage of all references to Brezhnev's last name. No use of "Comrade" title would give a score of 100 percent and indicate the maximum possible informality of relationship with Brezhnev. Scores for the three speeches combined range from an average of 50 percent per speech for Bodyul to slightly more than 2 percent for Usubaliyev.

"Total References." This is simply a count of all forms of reference to Brezhnev. Scores on this indicator are not adjusted for differences in length of speech. Most references to the Soviet leader cluster in the introductory or concluding portions of each speech, rather than in the bulky middle portion containing factual data on a region's performance, and total frequency of reference is not significantly related to length of speech. Efforts to adjust for length reduced, rather than enhanced, the apparent validity of the indicator.[6]

"Personal Praise." This is narrowly defined as praise for Brezhnev's qualities as a person and as a leader. Praise for his policies and for his report to the Party congress are not included, as with these forms of praise it is impossible to distinguish reliably between praise for Brezhnev personally and praise for the Party leadership collectively. Sentences containing personal praise were extracted from the speeches in a manner which concealed the identity of the speaker. These extracts were then ranked for degree of personal praise by three CIA Soviet analysts—not the same panel of analysts that had previously commented on the indicators. The analysts worked independently of each other but showed a high degree of agreement in their rankings.[7]

An indicator is valid to the extent that it actually measures what it purports to measure, in this case expressed support for Brezhnev. Unfortunately, there is no separate and sure measuring rod of actual support for Brezhnev against which to judge the scores on support for Brezhnev provided by the indicators. Lacking the ability to question the leaders and obtain straightforward answers on this subject, the researcher is faced with two options: to be content with theoretical justification of the indicators, or to seek some indirect means of checking their validity. We opted for the latter course. The best available independent criterion for judging these indicators is to ask the simple question, "How well do the results jibe with the informed judgment of analysts familiar with the Soviet political scene?"

The same panel of CIA analysts specializing in Soviet internal politics that commented on the indicators also ranked the sixteen leaders according to the leaders' support or lack of support for Brezhnev. The panelists' estimates of relative degree of support for Brezhnev were based on all available information about these leaders, not on their Party congress speeches. The three analysts prepared their rankings independently, and no effort was made to gain consensus among the analysts. Although the analysts were chosen from different offices in order to represent different perspectives, there was, nevertheless, a high measure of agreement between their rankings: Kendall's coefficient of concordance was 0.83. The separate rankings were averaged to form a single scale, a procedure which automatically compromised the differences between analysts. The panel's ranking of the sixteen leaders is presented in Table 2, p. 119.

Pearson's product moment correlation was used to relate the panel's average ranking of the sixteen leaders with the scores derived by applying each of the indicators to the three sets of speeches.[8] The higher the correlation between the average panel ranking and the scores based on an indicator, the greater the validity of the indicator as a measure of support for Brezhnev. This procedure assumes that the panel's ranking is correct (which, of course, may not be entirely true), but, as already noted, the informed judgment of knowledgeable analysts of the Soviet political scene is the best available standard for comparison.

An indicator is reliable to the degree that it gives the same results each time it is applied to the same or similar data, in this case the three speeches by one individual. Consistency is a synonym for reliability. Assuming, for example, that "Total References" to Brezhnev is a generally valid indicator, it would also be a reliable indicator only to the extent that those leaders who rank high on "Total References" in their regional congress speeches also rank high on this indicator in the Twenty-fifth Party Congress and regional *aktiv* speeches.

The measurement of reliability in this instance is quite imperfect because of differences in the context in which the three speeches were presented. In both the regional meetings, the leaders acted in Brezhnev's absence in their role as the top regional Party officials, as compared with the Twenth-fifth Party Congress when the regional leaders spoke in the role of subordinates in Brezhnev's presence. One would expect, therefore, that scores on both regional speeches should correlate with each other better than either regional speech correlates with the Twenty-fifth Party Congress speech, and this expectation is borne out by the data. Apart from this difference in presence or absence of Brezhnev, the context in which each leader gave his three speeches was very similar.

Measuring the reliability of a given indicator required calculating the correlation between three sets of speeches rather than only two. This was handled by computing the correlation for each of the three pairs of speeches and then averaging the results to arrive at the mean correlation.

TABLE 1

Indicators	Validity				Reliability
	Regional Congress	25th Party Congress	Regional Aktiv	Combined Ranking	
Leonid Ilich	.56*	.62**	.33	.68**	.37
Omitting Comrade	-.02	.57**	.62**	.64**	.21
Total References	.32	-.15	.30	.33	.28
Personal Praise	.52*	.12	.18	.33	.53*

Statistical Measures of Face Validity
and Reliability

*   Indicates statistical significance at the .05 level.
** Indicates statistical significance at the .01 level.

Testing the Indicators

Table 1 shows which indicators gave the most valid results, when validity is defined in terms of agreement with the panel's ranking. Statistically, the best indicators are "Leonid Il'ich" and "Omitting 'Comrade,'" with correlations of 0.68 and 0.64, respectively, both significant at the 0.01 level. Note that Table 1 shows the correlation between the scores on the indicators and the panel ranking for each of the three sets of speeches, as well as for the three sets of speeches combined, and that in some cases there is considerable disparity between speeches. This relative lack of consistency between speeches is reflected in the final column of this table, which shows the mean r (reliability) score. "Personal Praise" was clearly the most reliable indicator, with a mean r of 0.53.

"Leonid Il'ich" and "Omitting 'Comrade.'" The apparently strong validity of the "Leonid Il'ich" and "Omitting 'Comrade'" indicators is one of the more interesting revelations of this study. With the benefit of hindsight, it may seem self-evident that such informal modes of address would correlate highly with political support, but this was in fact an unexpected finding. Prior to analysis of the data, the panelists noted that Soviet use of first name and patronymic can not be equated with use of first name in Western culture. They judged that references to Leonid Il'ich and omission of "Comrade" were strongly influenced by a speaker's personal style and by linguistic and social conventions unrelated to the speaker's political support for Brezhnev. The strength of the correlations, however, offers persuasive evidence that both usages are in some way strongly influenced by the speaker's attitude toward or personal relationship with Brezhnev.[9]

One interpretation is that both indicators measure the degree of informality in the speaker's relationship with Brezhnev, and that informality in turn is closely related to support. Omitting "Comrade" indicates only informality, while use of first name and patronymic is a sign of both informality and a feeling of personal closeness. Leaders who rank high on "Omitting 'Comrade'" normally rank high on "Leonid Il'ich." Correlation between the two indicators is 0.85, which is significant at the 0.001 level and clearly suggests convergent validity. A distinction can be drawn between these two indicators, however, and it may be important to note when a leader ranks high on one but not the other. At the Twenty-fifth Party Congress, for example, Kosygin demonstrated the informality of his relationship with Brezhnev by invariably omitting "comrade," but he never expressed the affection normally associated with the use of first name and patronymic. This is as expected, given the longstanding working relationship but differing policy interests of the two leaders.

Degree of informality, as measured by the "Omitting 'Comrade'" indicator, is strongly influenced by Brezhnev's personal presence in the audience. At the Twenty-fifth Party Congress, speakers were addressing their remarks directly to Brezhnev as well as to the broader audience, and the Comrade title was omitted 35 percent of the time as compared with 18 percent and 15 percent when the leaders were speaking to their regional followers. In the aggregate, Brezhnev's presence prompts a more personal mode of reference. More importantly, however, Brezhnev's presence apparently requires that a speaker present a more accurate picture of his personal relationship with the general secretary. The data reveal a clear pattern that those regional leaders who are closest to Brezhnev were more informal, i.e., omitted "Comrade" more frequently, when speaking in Moscow in Brezhnev's presence than when speaking to their regional followers. Leaders who are least close to Brezhnev were more formal when speaking at the Twenty-fifth Party Congress than they were in their regional speeches.

It seems that leaders speaking in Brezhnev's presence seek to avoid offending him either by proclaiming an intimacy which does not in fact exist or by using fomal modes of reference when the relationship is perceived by Brezhnev as close and informal. Two conclusions follow from this. First, that "Omitting 'Comrade'" is a more valid indicator for speeches given in Brezhnev's presence than for other speeches, although it probably does have general validity as well. And second, the "Omitting 'Comrade'" and "Leonid

Il'ich" indicators are both far less susceptible to manipulation for political purposes than are the other indicators of political support for Brezhnev. Expressions of political support are more manipulable than a personal relationship. Brezhnev would welcome, and might respond favorably to, praise and political support from someone who had hitherto been cool to his leadership, but informality would be regarded as presumptuous when the relationship has actually been a formal one.[10]

"Total References." Public mention of any Soviet leader, either to praise him, to quote him as an authority, or to report on his activities, has long been recognized by Kremlinologists as an indication of support for that leader.[11] This form of support is measured by the "Total References" indicator. The combined score on "Total References," which is an average of rankings on the three sets of speeches, correlates with the average panel ranking with an r of 0.33, which is not statistically significant at the 0.05 level. Comparable analysis of speeches to the Twenty-fourth and Twenty-second Party Congresses confirms this relatively low validity. Reliability of the "Total References" indicator (mean r equals 0.28) also leaves a good deal to be desired.

The relatively low correlation between scores on "Total References" and the average panel ranking is possibly attributable to the influence of another variable—membership in the Politburo. Of the seven full or candidate Politburo members in the sample, six were clustered in the bottom half of the rankings on this indicator. Analysis of data for the Twenty-fourth and Twenty-second Party Congresses showed a somewhat similar pattern. It may be that for a different sample consisting entirely of Politburo members, or entirely of leaders not connected with that body, that the correlation between total references and support for Brezhnev would be much greater than for the mixed group analyzed here. The panelists had postulated that expression of political support would be related to political status, with those leaders whose political rank is closest to that of Brezhnev being most reserved in their expressions of support. This hypothesis seems to be confirmed by the "Total References" indicator, but as noted below it is not supported by the scores on "Personal Praise."

It is difficult to say to what extent Soviet leaders are consciously aware of the frequency with which they invoke Brezhnev's name in their speeches. It seems probable that Aliyev was well aware of what he was doing when he mentioned Brezhnev fifty-three times in his republic *aktiv* speech; one might even look for or speculate about what motivated him on this occasion to make twenty more references to Brezhnev than his nearest rival. In most cases, though, Soviet leaders may not pay much attention to whether they are invoking Brezhnev's name with marginally greater or lesser frequency than their colleagues or than in their own previous speeches. It is only sharp deviation from an established norm, or maintenance of a consistently high or low frequency over a prolonged period of time, that has analytical significance.

"Personal Praise." Praise is a salient indicator, and the one most heavily used by analysts of Soviet leaders' speeches to evaluate relative attitudes toward the General Secretary. As previously noted, the indicator "Personal Praise" as used here is narrowly defined as praise for Brezhnev's qualities as a person and as a leader, and it excludes praise for his policies or for his report to the Twenty-fifth Party Congress.

The relatively low correlation (r equals 0.33) between the rankings on the "Personal Praise" indicator and the average panel ranking is another surprising result of this study. Bodyul and Demirchyan, for example, who were ranked second and fifth by the panel, showed up as tenth and fifteenth on the "Personal Praise" indicator, while Grishkyavichus and Grishin were ranked twelfth and thirteenth by the panel but rose to third and fifth, respectively, on the indicator. Given the strong intuitive support for the validity of this indicator and its extensive use by analysts, the low correlation is disturbing and merits detailed examination.

There is reason to suspect that the low correlation is an anomaly attributable to some aspect of this particular group of speeches rather than to weaknesses in the indicator per se. Personal praise for Khrushchev at the Twenty-second Party Congress correlates with the average panel ranking for that Congress at 0.45, which is statistically significant at the 0.05 level. Similar ranking and statistical computation for the Twenty-fourth Party Congress was not feasible owing to insufficient personal praise at that congress; only six of the seventeen speeches analyzed contained any personal praise at all. The six leaders who did engage in personal praise of Brezhnev at the Twenty-fourth Party Congress coincided, however, with six of the top seven leaders in the panel ranking for that congress, and this is certainly a very strong correlation indeed.

Further, the reliability of the "Personal Praise" indicator (mean r equals 0.53) is far greater than for any of the other indicators, and it is the only one to reach statistical significance at the 0.05 level. This suggests that degree of personal praise in the three speeches at, or related to, the Twenty-fifth Party Congress must have been strongly influenced by some consistent motivational stimulus. Although personal praise in these speeches may not be a particularly good indicator of support for Brezhnev, the consistency in the use of personal praise over the three speeches indicates that it must be a good indicator of *something*.[12] These results seem to suggest a gap in our knowledge which, if filled, would then provide a key to interpretation of the data. As personal praise at the regional congresses alone correlates very well with the panel ranking (r equals 0.52), such a gap might just conceivably relate to leaders reacting differently to official guidelines concerning praise for Brezhnev at the Twenty-fifth Party Congress. There is some collateral evidence that the encomiums for Brezhnev at this congress were deemed excessive by some leaders, and that this became a subject of discussion within the leadership after the congress.

"Personal Relationship" and "Political Support." It is useful analytically to distinguish between two types of indicators—those that reveal something about a speaker's personal relationship with Brezhnev and those that tell something about expressed political support for Brezhnev. "Leonid Il'ich" and "Omitting 'Comrade'" are in the former category, while "Total References" and "Personal Praise" fall into the latter.

The "Leonid Il'ich" and "Omitting 'Comrade'" indicators are highly correlated (r equals 0.85) with each other and may be combined to form a composite indicator designated "Personal Relationship." This composite is formed by taking the mean of the rankings on the two individual indicators. "Personal Relationship" correlates extremely well with the average panel ranking, having an r of 0.70, which is significant at the 0.001 level. "Total References" and "Personal Support" has a 0.38 correlation with the average panel ranking, which is not significant at the 0.05 level. As the validity of this indicator is not established, any conclusions based upon it must be regarded as speculative, but it seems useful nonetheless to make certain comparisons between the "Personal Relationship" and "Political Support" indicators. These comparisons are shown in Table 2.

That "Personal Relationship" is far more highly correlated with the panel ranking than is "Political Support" is paradoxical, since the panel was asked to rank the leaders on political support for Brezhnev, *not* personal relationship.

TABLE 2

	Panel Ranking	Personal Relationship	Political Support
Kunayev	1	2.5	8
Bodyul	2	4	6
Shcherbitsky	3	6	9
Aliyev	4	2.5	1
Demirchyan	5	10	11
Shevardnadze	6	1	2
Romanov	7	9	13
Rashidov	8	5	7
Usubaliyev	9	16	5
Gapurov	10	11	16
Rasulov	11	8	4
Grishkyavichus	12	13	3
Grishin	13	7	10
Voss	14.5	15	12
Kebin	14.5	12	14
Masherov	16	14	15

Comparison of Panel Ranking with Ranking on *Personal Relationship* and *Political Support* Indicators, Based on Combined Scores for Three 1976 Speeches.

There are at least two reasons for the better correlation with "Personal Relationship." One is that the indicators of political support may be strongly influenced by topical political developments or be manipulated for transitory political goals, whereas the panel ranking and the components of the "Personal Relationship" indicator both focus on more stable factors. The second, and perhaps more important, reason is that personal relationship with a leader is a very strong determinant of political support for that leader, especially in the Soviet Union, and in preparing its rankings the panel weighed known patronage relationships higher than public statements of support. Thus, known or assumed personal relationships had a significant impact on the panel's rankings.

For example, Shcherbitsky, a known Brezhnev protegé, was ranked high by the panel even though panelists were aware that his public statements of support for Brezhnev have been rather reserved. This disparity between Shcherbitsky's strong personal relationship with Brezhnev and relatively weak expression of political support for him is reflected in the scores on the indicators. Demirchyan, too, was ranked relatively high by the panel despite his observed reticence in praise for Brezhnev, because it was assumed that his recent appointment as Armenian First Secretary indicated a patronage relationship to Brezhnev. Demirchyan's below-average ranking on both "Personal Relationship" and "Political Support" indicators suggests that he may actually owe his appointment to some leader other than Brezhnev and, thus, that the panel ranking of him may be incorrect.

The comparison of ranking on "Personal Relationship" with ranking on "Political Support," as shown in Table 2, reveals several interesting relationships. In most cases, leaders rank similarly on both types of indicators. Divergence between the two suggests a need for closer examination and explanation. Usubaliyev and Grishkyavichus both rank low on

"Personal Relationship" but high on "Political Support"—there is a difference of eleven and ten ranks, respectively. Although their personal relationship with Brezhnev is distant, these two leaders appear to be actively seeking his favor expressing support for his leadership. This effort to improve their status vis-à-vis Brezhnev suggests that they may feel insecure in the positions, and that they are seeking to overcome or compensate for their relatively distant personal relationship. This distinguishes Usubaliyev and Grishkyavichus from other leaders who rank low on indicators of "Personal Relationship" but who also rank low on "Political Support." These other leaders appear to be content with their current status, presumably because they feel secure with the patronage of some top leader other than Brezhnev. If this analysis is correct, it seems clear that the "Political Support" indicator measures desired support *from* Brezhnev as well as support *for* Brezhnev.

Conclusions

Kremlinological analysis is based on the assumption that Soviet leaders in major speeches choose their words with care, and that small differences in wording may convey significant differences in meaning. This research has tested some limits of that assumption. What differences in references to Brezhnev have meaning, and how much meaning under what circumstances? An unanticipated finding was that reference to Brezhnev by his first name and patronymic, and omission of "Comrade" when referring to Brezhnev, are both strong indicators of support for the Soviet leader. Personal praise and total number of references to Brezhnev were also identified as useful indicators, albeit with limitations that make them less valid than had been expected.

The accuracy of our analysis depends heavily upon the

accuracy of the ranking of the sixteen leaders by the panel of analysts, for this is the standard against which the indicators were judged. We adopted this standard not just because it was the only criterion available, but because these analysts do possess a current, in-depth knowledge of Soviet politics. To be believable, the result of our empirical analysis had to be generally consistent with the analysts' prior judgment about these leaders. To be useful, it had to add new and believable detail to this existing picture. The procedure used here passed both tests.[13]

The consistency of leaders' rankings on three of the four indicators was rather low. This is partially attributable to Brezhnev's presence during one set of speeches and his absence during the other two. Since the occasion, audience and political context of the three speeches were about as similar as one can reasonably expect to find, however, it had been hoped that a leader who ranked high relative to the other leaders on one indicator for one speech would also rank high on that same indicator for his other two speeches. That this hope was often unfulfilled suggests either that the context of the three speeches was not as similar as it appeared to be, or that, in most cases, the leaders in preparing their speeches did not exercise conscious control over the indicators analyzed here. A leader has certain underlying tendencies, but the extent to which these get expressed in any given speech in a form measured by the indicators depends upon a number of other variables. Valid conclusions require a sample of speeches sufficiently large to offset this variation between individual speeches.

The principal goal of this study was to test the indicators, but it also generated, as a by-product, extensive data on the individual leaders. Change in overall support for Brezhnev or in the relative position of individual leaders assumes greater importance as the succession looms closer. This study established benchmarks for the detection and measurement of such changes.[14] And once Brezhnev has passed from the scene, there will be a pressing need to assess the standing and the sources of support for the new Party leader. The methodology employed here for organizing and analyzing voluminous data concerning references to the top leader can be useful for that purpose.

Further research in two directions seems warranted. The indicators need to be further validated with a larger sample of leaders and different speeches over time, so that the effects of other variables, such as date of speech and political rank, may be more precisely determined and taken into account in drawing inferences from the data. Rather than rank-ordering a specified group of leaders, it is necessary to develop an absolute scale and a coefficient of support for the Party leader. A regression equation could then be used to weight the content analytic data according to date of speech and other potentially relevant variables, and to determine where each speaker falls on the scale of support for the General Secretary.

If a coefficient of support for the General Secretary could be assigned reliably to every Soviet official who makes a sufficient number of public speeches, it would then be possible to analyze systematically the relationship between support for the top leader and the other variables commonly included in studies of Soviet elites. One could, for example, ask questions such as the following: Is support for Brezhnev influenced by career experience, generational grouping, or ethnic origin? How important is support for Brezhnev in determining who gets promoted? And when Brezhnev is succeeded by another leader, which individuals or elite groups give greater or lesser support to the new leader as compared with their support for Brezhnev?

Notes

1. An *aktiv* is composed of leading Party members from all important institutions. Its meetings are used principally to discuss and disseminate information.

2. Analysis is based on English translations as provided by the Foreign Broadcast Information Service (FBIS) *Daily Report* for the regional and Twenty-fifth Party Congress speeches, and by the Joint Publications Research Series, *Translations on the USSR: Political and Sociological Affairs*, supplemented by the FBIS *Daily Report*, for the speeches to the regional *aktivs*.

3. Of course, a speech by a public figure may tell as much about the anonymous writer who prepared it as about the leader who delivered it. The speeches selected for analysis here, however, are far from routine; they are among the most important speeches these Soviet leaders will give during their political careers. Initial drafts were probably prepared by speechwriters, but those writers will have followed the style and policy guidelines of their bosses. It seems certain that each leader will have carefully edited and personalized each speech. For the type of analysis done here, any speech as important as those selected for this study can and should be regarded as the personal expession of the leader who gives it.

4. Myron Rush, *The Rise of Khrushchev* (Washington, D.C.: Public Affairs Press, 1958), p. 89.

5. The five additional indicators not discussed in this report are the following: number of specific policies associated with Brezhnev's name; reference to the principal report to the Twenty-fifth Party Congress as "Brezhnev's report" versus reference to it as the "CPSU Central Committee report delivered by Brezhnev"; reference to the Politburo without mention of Brezhnev's name; use of the phrase "the Politburo headed by Brezhnev"; and reference to "Brezhnev personally," as in the phrase "the Central Committee, its Politburo, and Leonid Il'ich Brezhnev . . . personally."

6. Coding of these first three indicators is a mechanical process of word identification that does not require the exercise of coder judgment. Intercoder reliability was, therefore, very high. The Twenty-fifth Party Congress speeches were coded for these indicators by both the author and his research assistant with an intercoder reliability of 0.97.

7. Kendall's coefficient of concordance is an appropriate statistical

procedure for measuring the agreement between rankings prepared by three or more judges. The coefficients for the three sets of speeches were 0.90, 0.94, and 0.86, each of which indicates a very acceptable degree of agreement. There is, of course, some potential for error in the author's selection of extracts to be ranked by the analysts. No significant ambiguities were encountered in making the selections, however. This is thought to have had very slight influence, if any at all, on how the leaders were ranked.

8. Spearman's *r* was also applied with essentially the same results.

9. Evidence from the Twenty-fourth and Twenty-second Party Congresses was less clearcut; correlations for "Omitting 'Comrade'" were 0.54 and 0.15, respectively. Insufficient frequency of use of first name and patronymic precluded statistical analysis of the "Leonid Il'ich" indicator for these Congresses.

10. Indicators of personal relationship can also be manipulated under certain circumstances, however. It seems highly unlikely, for example, that any of these indicators would successfully penetrate a deliberate conspiracy such as toppled Khrushchev in 1964.

11. For example, see Franz Borkenau, "Getting at the Facts Behind the Facade," *Commentary* 17, no. 4 (April 1954): 397.

12. The panelists hypothesized that higher praise is to be expected from lower echelon leaders than from those whose status is more nearly equal to that of Brezhnev, and that higher praise is also anticipated from Central Asian leaders than from leaders representing areas less dependent upon Moscow's largesse. Neither hypothesis was supported by the available data on this indicator. It was not possible to measure the degree to which "Personal Praise" was influenced by personality characteristics.

13. There is, of course, a certain circularity in using the analysts' subjective judgment about the leaders to validate the indicators and then using the indicators, in turn, to evaluate and refine and deepen the analysts' judgments. It is our contention, however, that such a reciprocal relationship between judgment and data is fundamental to all empirical analysis. Selection of indicators is always a judgmental process, with these judgments subject to reappraisal based on the data analysis. In the present study, the fact that two wholly independent measures (panel ranking and "Personal Relationship" indicator) of the same phenomenon (support for Brezhnev) correlate so highly supports the validity of both measurements. The convergence between the measure-

ments is evidence that both procedures are indeed measuring the same thing.

14. The data in tabular form organized by leader as well as by indicator and by speech is available from the author.

7

An Events Data Base for Analysis
of Transnational Terrorism

Edward F. Mickolus

A computerized data base, called ITERATE (an acronym for International Terrorism: Attributes of Terrorist Events), was developed as a pilot project to permit a more systematic study of the phenomenon of transnational terrorism. By recording all available information on terrorism in a form that makes it retrievable and manipulable by computer, it becomes possible to discover, document, and analyze patterns in the behavior of terrorists, while recognizing the possibility of idiosyncratic deviation by the perpetrators of specific events. This paper describes the ITERATE data base and how it may be used.

Some definitional preliminaries are an essential part of any empirical investigation. It is necessary to define transnational terrorism in order to determine what events to include in, and exclude from, the data base. Unfortunately, definitions of terrorism vary greatly among governments, private research corporations, and academic researchers. For purposes of this project, we have defined terrorism in general as

This chapter is adapted from an article by the same author entitled "Statistical Approaches to the Study of Terrorism" previously published in Yonah Alexander and Seymour Maxwell Finger, eds., *Terrorism: Interdisciplinary Perspectives* (New York: John Jay, 1977).

the use, or threat of use, of anxiety-inducing extranormal violence for political purposes, when such action is intended to
influence the attitudes and behavior of a target group wider
than that of the immediate victims.

The concept of terrorism can be further refined by using
location and nature of the perpetrators to identify four kinds
of terrorism, as described below. The data base is limited to
one of these four types, transnational terrorism.

Transnational terrorism, our subject of inquiry, includes
terrorist actions carried out by basically autonomous non-
state actors, whether or not they enjoy some degree of moral
or material support from sympathetic governments, and
which involve the nationals or territory of some foreign
country. Examples include the kidnappings of diplomats and
businessmen overseas, the skyjacking of international flights,
embassy barricade-and-hostage episodes, etc.

Interstate terrorism includes terrorist acts carried out by
individuals or groups controlled by the governmental authority of a sovereign state, when these acts involve the nationals
or territory of some other country. Examples include the
campaign conducted by Spanish authorities against Basque
nationalists in France, attacks against Palestinian groups in
Europe and the Middle East by Israeli intelligence agents, etc.
Acts of interstate terrorism are not included in the data base.

Domestic terrorism confines itself to the nationals and
territory of only one state. It is the domestic parallel to transnational terrorism in that it is carried on by basically autonomous nonstate actors, but only affects citizens of one state.
Examples include bombings by the IRA and UDA within the
borders of Northern Ireland, Weather Underground bombings
in New York, and attempted assassination of governmental
leaders by nationals of their own country.

State terrorism includes terrorist actions conducted by a
national government within the borders of its own country; it

FIGURE 1

TYPES OF POLITICAL TERRORISM

Direct Involvement of Nationals or
Territory of More than One State?

		Yes	No
Government Controlled	Yes	Interstate	State
or Directed?	No	Transnational	Domestic

is the domestic equivalent of interstate terrorism. Examples include Soviet purges in the 1930s, and police state torture.

Given that it is transnational terrorist behavior that is to be explained, how can this phenomenon be investigated empirically? We could engage in a review of the literature of terrorism, reading *inter alia* books on the art of guerrilla warfare by prominent practitioners. We might also ask terrorists about their behavior, interviewing either those imprisoned or still in the field.[1] We may, however, be led astray by the terrorists' attempts to propagandize their cause through our efforts, and terrorists may also be unaware of constraints on their own behavior.

As a check on conclusions based upon these other forms of research, we could also observe terrorist behavior itself, rather than statements about such behavior. This is the approach taken by the ITERATE project, which focuses on the individual terrorist incident. In the pilot version of the data set, 107 distinct descriptors of an incident were used to give a snapshot of approximately 500 terrorist incidents reported in the initial RAND chronology of international terrorist incidents from 1968 to 1974.[2] Terms used to describe incidents verbally were coded into machine-readable numeric forms. Characteristics of incidents such as the type of attack, the location, the identity and nationality of the victims of the attack and the targets of the demands of the terrorists, the types and extent of demands made, and the outcomes (damage, casualties, governmental responses) of the incident can thus be quickly summarized in a centrally available data pool.[3] See Appendix for a listing of ITERATE variables and values.[4]

Applications

ITERATE is a research tool. An appreciation of the way this tool may be used is afforded by the following examples of its use to summarize trends, compare terrorist campaigns cross-nationally and over time, evalute policy prescriptions for crisis management, and support incident negotiations.

Trends in Transnational Terrorism

Table 1 shows annual trends in the types of transnational attacks which have been experienced worldwide.[5] The attempted taking of hostages (i.e. barricade-and-hostage, kidnappings, nonair takeovers, and skyjackings) has become a popular tactic among terrorists, and the probability that the hostage-takers will successfully seize a hostage has grown dramatically since the beginning of the 1970s. Despite the publicity given to isolated incidents of aerial hijacking, the improvements made in security procedures in 1973, bilateral extradition or prosecution treaties, as well as the unwillingness of governments to grant asylum have led to a dramatic decrease in this type of incident.[6] Purely destructive acts, such as bombing of facilities and assassinations, are unfortunately on the rise.[7]

Table 2 shows steady rises in injuries and total casualties,

TABLE 1

INTERNATIONAL TERRORIST INCIDENTS, 1968-1975

Incident Type	1968	1969	1970	1971	1972	1973	1974	1975	Total
Kidnapping	1	4	31	17	11	34	31	32	161
Barricade & Hostage	0	0	2	1	4	8	12	17	44
Skyjacking	33	80	70	37	38	19	11	6	294
Takeover of Non-Air Transportation	0	0	3	0	1	0	1	1	6
Bombing	38	82	83	71	74	93	147	78	666
Letterbomb	2	2	2	2	222	50	6	3	289
Armed Attack	2	7	8	12	4	10	12	10	65
Murder or Assassination	7	5	12	8	7	14	11	19	83
Arson or Molotov Cocktail	0	14	21	10	1	15	13	6	80
Theft or Break-in	3	7	13	2	1	1	2	3	32
Sabotage	0	0	0	1	3	0	1	0	5
Total	86	201	245	161	366	244	247	175	1,725
Total Without Letterbomb[8]	84	199	243	159	144	194	241	172	1,436

[8] Defining what constitutes a letterbomb incident hinges upon what is accepted as the location of the attack. For example, an individual terrorist may mail two letterbombs from Country A to Countries B and C. If we define the location of mailing as the location of the incident, only one incident is counted. If, however, we note the destination of the letterbombs, two incidents would be counted. Using the second definition may give an inflated impression of terrorists initiatives, but the tracing of exploded letterbombs to the scene of the mailing, and to an individual, is extremely difficult. In the table, the final destination criterion is employed. To offset the possible inflationary effect, total incidents are calculated with and without letterbombs.

TABLE 2

ANNUAL CASUALTIES FROM TERRORIST ACTIONS
(INCLUDES TERRORISTS, POLICE, FOREIGN AND
DOMESTIC NON-COMBATANTS)

Year	Killed	Wounded	Total
1968	12	36	48
1969	16	98	114
1970	104	135	239
1971	39	242	281
1972	154	321+	475+
1973	119+	477	596+
1974	375	936	1,311
1975	155	469	624
Total	974	2,714	3,688

with deaths due to terrorist actions showing a more erratic
increase. Indiscriminate selection of victims appears to have
added greatly to the casualty totals, although most attacks
appear to still be aimed at individuals or institutions with
symbolic value.

Cross-National Comparisons

High-speed transportation greatly enhances the operational capabilities of transnational terrorists. We are often
told that terrorists are now able to strike virtually anywhere
in the world. Has this capability been used? What have been
the sites of operations? Table 3 gives us some idea of the

TABLE 3

LOCATION OF INCIDENT, BY COUNTRY, REGION, AND TYPE

Location	B&H	Sky-jack	Kid-nap	Murder	Armed Attack	Bombs	Letter Bombs	Arson
ATLANTIC COMMUNITY								
Austria	2	1	–	1	–	3	–	1
Belgium	–	–	–	1	–	12	3	2
Canada	–	2	2	1	–	4	3	–
Cyprus	–	–	–	2	2	1	–	–
Denmark	–	–	1	1	–	4	–	–
France	4	5	4	8	4	29	3	2
Gibraltar	–	–	–	–	–	–	1	–
Greece	2	5	–	1	2	38	–	–
Ireland	–	2	2	2	–	8	1	1
Italy	–	5	2	4	–	24	1	10
Netherlands	4	1	–	–	–	6	–	2
Northern Ireland	–	–	2	1	5	8	–	1
Norway	–	–	–	1	–	1	–	–
Portugal	–	1	–	–	–	2	1	–
Spain	1	2	3	4	–	3	–	3
Sweden	2	1	–	1	–	6	–	–
Switzerland	–	3	–	–	1	4	7	–
W. Germany	1	6	1	4	3	21	1	10
UK	3	2	1	4	1	81	34+	3
US	–	98	–	6	5	114	11	10
MIDDLE EAST								
Algeria	1	1	–	–	–	–	1	–
Bahrain	–	1	–	–	–	–	–	–
Dubai	–	2	–	–	–	–	–	–
Egypt	–	5	–	1	1	–	4	–
Iran	–	2	1	4	–	4	–	–
Iraq	–	1	–	–	–	–	–	–
Israel	6	1	1	1	10	28	2	3
Jordan	1	2	3	4	1	7	4	1
Kuwait	1	–	–	1	–	–	–	–
Lebanon	1	10	11	4	10	25	7	2
Libya	–	1	–	–	–	–	1	–
Morocco	–	–	–	–	–	2	–	–
Saudi Arabia	–	–	–	–	–	1	–	–
Sudan	1	–	–	–	–	1	–	–
Syria	–	–	–	1	–	3	–	–
Tunisia	1	–	–	–	–	–	–	–
Turkey	–	3	4	–	1	25	1	4
Yemen	–	2	–	–	–	–	–	–

TABLE 3 continued

LOCATION OF INCIDENT, BY COUNTRY, REGION, AND TYPE

Location	B&H	Sky-jack	Kid-nap	Murder	Armed Attack	Bombs	Letter Bombs	Arson
LATIN AMERICA								
Argentina	1	8	44	5	5	119	1	3
Bahamas	—	1	—	1	—	—	—	—
Bolivia	—	1	4	—	—	4	—	2
Brazil	—	8	8	5	—	.3	1	4
British Honduras	—	1	—	—	—	—	—	—
Chile	—	2	—	—	—	5	1	—
Colombia	—	24	5	2	1	2	—	—
Costa Rica	—	2	—	—	—	—	—	—
Cuba	—	1	—	—	1	—	1	—
Dominican Republic	1	2	2	—	—	2	—	—
Ecuador	—	6	—	—	—	5	1	—
El Salvador	—	—	—	—	—	3	—	—
Guatemala	—	—	5	3	—	1	—	—
Haiti	1	—	—	—	—	1	—	—
Honduras	—	1	—	—	—	1	—	—
Jamaica	—	1	—	—	—	2	—	—
Mexico	1	11	6	—	1	19	—	—
Netherlands Antilles	—	1	—	—	—	—	—	—
Nicaragua	1	1	—	—	—	—	—	—
Panama	—	1	—	—	—	—	—	1
Paraguay	—	—	1	1	—	—	—	—
Peru	—	1	—	—	—	5	1	1
Puerto Rico	—	3	—	—	—	6	—	—
Uruguay	—	1	10	—	2	3	—	—
Venezuela	—	6	2	—	1	1	—	—
AFRICA								
Angola	—	2	3	—	—	—	—	—
Botswana	—	—	—	—	—	—	1	—
Chad	—	—	1	—	—	—	—	—
Ethiopia	—	4	13	2	1	1	—	—
Kenya	—	1	—	—	—	—	—	—
Mozambique	—	—	2	—	—	—	—	—
Rhodesia	—	—	—	—	—	—	1	—
Somalia	—	—	1	—	—	—	—	—

TABLE 3 continued

LOCATION OF INCIDENT, BY COUNTRY, REGION, AND TYPE

Location	B&H	Sky-jack	Kid-nap	Murder	Armed Attack	Bombs	Letter Bombs	Arson
AFRICA continued								
South Africa	1	1	1	—	—	—	2	—
Spanish Sahara	—	—	1	—	—	—	—	—
Tanzania	—	—	1	1	—	—	1	—
Uganda	—	—	1	—	—	—	—	—
Zaire	—	—	—	—	—	—	2	—
Zambia	—	—	—	—	—	1	2	—
ASIA								
Afghanistan	—	—	—	1	—	—	—	—
Australia	—	2	—	—	—	7	—	2
Bangladesh	1	—	—	1	—	1	—	—
Burma	—	—	1	—	—	—	—	—
Cambodia	—	—	—	—	—	3	—	—
India	—	3	—	—	—	4	55	—
Japan	—	2	—	1	1	3	—	6
Malaysia	1	—	—	—	—	—	35	—
Nepal	—	1	—	—	—	—	—	1
New Zealand	—	—	—	—	—	1	—	1
Pakistan	1	—	—	1	1	2	—	—
Philippines	1	4	2	2	—	8	—	—
Singapore	—	—	—	—	—	—	—	1
South Korea	—	2	—	1	—	—	—	—
S. Vietnam	—	3	—	—	—	—	—	—
Thailand	1	1	1	1	—	—	—	—
EAST EUROPE								
Czechoslo-vakia	—	6	—	—	—	—	—	—
Finland	—	1	—	—	—	—	—	—
Poland	—	4	—	—	—	—	—	—
Romania	—	2	—	—	—	—	—	—
USSR	—	5	—	—	—	—	—	—
Yugoslavia	—	—	—	—	—	—	—	1

major patterns.[8]

Conventional wisdom seems to be that most terrorism occurs in the emerging nations of the Third World. While this may be true for domestic terrorism, however, it does not appear to be the case with transnational actions. Nearly half of the incidents reported from 1968 to 1975 occurred in what are considered to be Westernized, highly affluent nations (42 percent of the total of all incidents occurred in Atlantic Community nations—46 percent if we exclude letter bombs). On the other hand, Eastern European nations have been relatively immune to attacks, suffering only sporadic skyjackings by dissidents. Latin America and the Middle East share second place to the Western nations as sites of attacks, whereas Asia and Africa experience such incidents infrequently. Middle Eastern terrorist groups have not developed the undergrounds that are necessary to attack certain types of targets (e.g., some other groups have needed up to fifty individuals to support a kidnapping operation). Additionally, there are few Israeli diplomatic or military installations available in the area, and few kidnap prospects. Hence, we do not find certain types of incidents on Middle Eastern soil to the extent which one would otherwise expect. Rather, Arab terrorists have gone abroad and resorted to the barricade-and-hostage scenario.

Transnational terrorism as a threat to Western security appears greater if we consider the nationality of the victims of attack (shown in Table 4), rather than the location of the incident. While it is still true that no nation can consider itself completely safe, and that many nations have suffered from transnational threats and incidents, the overwhelming majority of assaults are aimed at citizens of the industrialized Western nations. Atlantic Community citizens suffered in 63 percent of all incidents, while the United States has seen its nationals victimized in fully 36 percent of all cases of transnational terrorism. Again, we find that transnational terrorism is an oddity rather than a serious problem for Africans and Asians, with Eastern Europeans suffering only occasional assaults. In the Middle East, it is not surprising to find the Israelis the most harassed, with nationals of the more moderate Arab nations also being singled out for attack. Latin American guerrillas frequently involve non-Latins as victims, with those perceived to be rich capitalist exploiters often being selected.

In general, the Third World nationals who are victimized are most often ambassadors, or managers of a multinational corporation's local subsidiary. Hence, although nationals of any country may be subject to the occasional terrorist incident abroad, Western citizens face the highest probability of being the latest headline. Cross-tabulation of the ITERATE data to show vicitimization by location may aid the security offices in various foreign affairs ministries in determining the priorities for their overseas protection budgets.

Policy Prescriptions

In recent years, members of the U.S. Cabinet Committee to Combat Terrorism, police negotiations experts, think-tank researchers, and interested academics have debated the question of granting concessions to terrorists during hostage situations.[9] Will terrorists be deterred from future attacks if they are unable to obtain what they are demanding? Will other groups copy the successful tactics of terrorists who obtain concessions? What are the terrorists seeking in such incidents? How should negotiations be conducted even if a no-concessions policy is to be followed? Are there any identifiable patterns of behavior of individuals faced with this type of bargaining relationship?

It is the position of the U.S. State Department that we

TABLE 4

VICTIMS OF TERRORIST ACTIONS,
BY NATIONALITY AND REGION

	Number of Incidents			Number of Incidents
NORTH ATLANTIC			**ASIA** continued	
Austria	7		North Korea	1
Belgium	7		Pakistan	1
Canada	13		P.R. China	1
Cyprus	1		Philippines	8
Denmark	3		Singapore	2
France	39		South Korea	4
Greece	20		South Vietnam	4
Holy See	2		Taiwan	1
Ireland	15		Thailand	1
Italy	54			
Netherlands	17		**AFRICA**	
Portugal	9			
Spain	54		Angola	1
Sweden	5		Ethiopia	14
Switzerland	15		Gabon	1
West Germany	40		Ivory Coast	1
United			Kenya	1
Kingdom	173		Liberia	1
United States	616		Malawi	1
			Mozambique	4
ASIA			Nigeria	1
			Rhodesia	2
Australia	6		Senegal	1
Bangladesh	1		South Africa	9
Hong Kong	1		Tanzania	1
India	11		Zaire	1
Indonesia	4			
Japan	12		**LATIN AMERICA**	
Malaysia	1			
Nepal	1		Argentina	28
New Zealand	1		Bahamas	5

TABLE 4 continued

VICTIMS OF TERRORIST ACTIONS, BY NATIONALITY AND REGION

	Number of Incidents		Number of Incidents
LATIN AMERICA continued		**MIDDLE EAST** continued	
Bolivia	5		
Brazil	16	Jordan	26
British		Kuwait	3
Honduras	1	Lebanon	27
British West		Libya	2
Indies	1	Morocco	1
Chile	15	Palestinians	24
Colombia	30	Qatar	1
Costa Rica	3	Saudi Arabia	10
Cuba	21	South Yemen	1
Dominican		Syria	4
Republic	7	Turkey	12
Ecuador	9	United Arab Emirates	1
Guatemala	1	Yemen	
Haiti	3		
Honduras	2	**EAST EUROPE**	
Jamaica	1		
Mexico	15	Albania	1
Netherlands		Czechoslovakia	8
Antilles	2	East Germany	1
Nicaragua	3	Finland	1
Panama	4	Poland	9
Paraguay	3	Romania	2
Peru	5	USSR	33
Puerto Rico	9	Yugoslavia	26
Uruguay	11		
Venezuela	13	**OTHER**	
MIDDLE EAST		CENTO	3
		NATO	1
Algeria	8	OAS	2
Dubai	1	UN	1
Egypt	16	Foreigners (i.e.,	31
Iran	9	source inspecific	
Iraq	5	about nationality	
Israel	119	af victim	

should be willing to talk with the hostage-takers, but never give in to extortionate demands for the release of our nationals. Has this policy been successful in deterring future attacks? The answer is unclear. In Table 5, we note that the U.S. government is very rarely the target of explicit demands (e.g., monetary ransom, release of prisoners, etc.), suggesting a successful policy of deterrence. U.S. citizens, however, still remain the most popular kidnap subjects. It appears that American citizens are chosen for other reasons than as pawns in negotiations with the U.S. government. The terrorists may believe, for example, that they can negotiate directly with the victim's corporation. They may also believe that the target government may be more willing to grant concessions for a U.S. citizen than for one of its own. They may also believe that the U.S. government would be willing to apply pressure upon the target government to obtain the safe release of the American at whatever cost.

One may also question whether the terrorists engage in hostage-taking solely out of the expectation that their stated demands will be satisfied. In Table 6, we note that not all of the incidents can be characterized as aiming at securing money or prisoner release. A host of other publicly stated motivations have been given, and even more can be suggested if we look at terrorism as a general strategy, rather than focusing on the isolated incident. The group may be attempting to achieve publicity for their cause and may consider the government's acceding to their demands as merely a bonus effect. The terrorists may be hoping that the government does not give in to their demands, so that they may point out the lack of charity of the government in not distributing food to the people, or the government's inability to release prisoners who were secretly murdered in torture chambers, etc. It may well be the case, to paraphrase Ernest Evans of MIT, that the relationship of the no-concessions position to deter-

TABLE 5

NATIONALITY OF TARGETS OF DEMANDS, BY NATION, REGION, AND MULTIPLICITY OF TARGETS

Target of Demands	Number of Incidents Involving Only One Target	Number of Incidents Involving More Than One Target	Total
ATLANTIC COMMUNITY			
Austria	1	0	1
Canada	2	0	2
France	3	2	5
Greece	5	0	5
Ireland	1	0	1
Italy	1	0	1
Netherlands	0	2	2
Spain	1	0	1
Sweden	1	1	2
Switzerland	0	4	4
Turkey	4	0	4
United Kingdom	1	5	6
United States	2	2	4
West Germany	4	8	12
LATIN AMERICA			
Argentina	2	1	3
Bolivia	1	1	2
Brazil	4	0	4
Colombia	1	0	1
Dominican Republic	3	0	3
Guatemala	4	0	4
Haiti	1	0	1
Mexico	3	0	3
Nicaragua	2	0	2
Uruguay	4	0	4
Venezuela	1	0	1

continued

TABLE 5 continued

NATIONALITY OF TARGETS OF DEMANDS, BY NATION, REGION, AND MULTIPLICITY OF TARGETS

Target of Demands	Number of Incidents Involving Only One Target	Number of Incidents Involving More Than One Target	Total
MIDDLE EAST			
Algeria	0	1	1
Egypt	1	2	3
Israel	7	2	9
Jordan	2	2	4
Kuwait	0	1	1
Lebanon	0	1	1
Saudi Arabia	0	1	1
ASIA			
Burma	1	0	1
India	2	0	2
Japan	1	2	3
Philippines	3	0	3
Singapore	1	0	1
Thailand	0	1	1
OTHER			
South Africa	1	0	1
Tanzania	0	1	1
Yugoslavia	1	0	1
PPLP Terrorists	1	0	1
Corporations	25	5	31
Target not specified	28	0	28

TABLE 6

TERRORISTS' PUBLICLY STATED MOTIVATIONS FOR ACTIONS

Stated Demands or Motivations	Barricade & Hostage	Kidnapping	Aerial Hijacking
Release political prisoners (only)	13	25	16
Monetary ransom (only)	1	47	7
Release prisoners and monetary ransom	3	9	5
Publish manifesto	0	10	1
No demands mentioned	0	18	1
Questioning and/or instruction of hostages	0	6	0
Retaliation	0	2	4
Other (including free passage from scene of incident, specific political changes)	14	15	9

rence is not one of success or effectiveness, but rather one of irrelevance.[10]

One often hears that governments should attempt to get at the root causes of terrorism, rather than fighting its symptoms. Cures for the ills of the nation are what is called for, rather than tighter security measures. But what are the causes of terrorism? Do they lie with the individual, the group, or characteristics of the nation? Why are some nations singled out as victims, others as targets of demands? Why do some nations breed terrorist groups, whereas others that are apparently similar have been relatively free from being such greenhouses of violence? Why have some nations been chosen as sites for attacks? Systematic cross-national research on the characteristics of nations, comparing them on national wealth, political institutions and political participation, feelings of relative deprivation on the part of the populace, legal systems, etc., using ITERATE as a partial index of levels of transnational terrorism, may aid in answering these questions and developing preventive measures.

Crisis Management Support

When a U.S. citizen is kidnapped by unknown persons, our local embassy receives a message from a group purporting to hold our national hostage, demanding ransom and prisoner release to secure his safety. How do we know this claim is not a hoax? Once we have established its reliability, how do we deal with the incident? What do we know about the behavior of this group in similar situations? Will it hold to its part of the bargain? Will our hostage be killed during negotiations? Can we get the group to extend its deadline? What are the group's relations with the government, other groups, and to the population?

ITERATE can serve as a tool for tactical analytical support to the team managing the U.S. response to a terrorist incident. By comparing its large files of cases of actual kidnappings with instances of hoaxes, we can note systematic differences between the two and be led to a better decision about the credibility of a current message. Is the group claiming responsibility one which has surfaced previously? Is the name being used as a "cover" name for some other group that wishes to maintain "plausible denial" in the event of public revulsion at the outcome of the incident? Has the group claiming responsibility for the incident engaged in this type of action before? If not, are there any reasons to believe that it would have added this tactic to its repertoire? Further analysis of the group's profile through use of other ITERATE descriptive variables can lead to tentative answers to these questions.

Conclusion

ITERATE was a pilot project developed by the author while he was a CIA summer intern. Owing to limitations in the data in the system, it was not intended for broad use within the intelligence and policymaking communities and has not been so used, although it has provided statistics for a major CIA study on terrorism.[11] It has also been used in other government-sponsored research to test hypotheses about deterrence and the effects of publicity on terrorist behavior, and to devise general profiles of terrorist behavior in hostage bargaining situations.

As a pilot project, the purpose of ITERATE was to demonstrate the feasibility and utility of such a data base, and it has achieved this objective. Work is now proceeding within CIA and other agencies to develop more advanced systems, and members of the intelligence and policy communities have expressed interest in using the concepts and techniques employed in ITERATE in designing a community-wide data set.

Appendix: ITERATE Incident Coding Scheme

Each terrorist incident in the ITERATE data base is coded using the following 107 descriptors.*

Descriptor   Descriptor Name

1   DATE OF START OF INCIDENT month day year

2   CODE NUMBER. Four-digit number to be used for quick access to each discrete incident

3   TYPE OF EVENT

    1 kidnapping

    2 seizure--barricade and hostage

    3 seizure--occupation without hostages

    4 bombing--letter/parcel bombs

    5 bombing--arson/Molotov cocktail

    6 planted bomb--single detonation

    7 planted bomb--booby-trap detonation after initial explosion

    8 armed attack-missiles

    9 armed attack--other weapons, e.g., sniping, machine-gunning

    10 skyjacking

    11 takeover of non-aerial means of transportation

    12 assassination/murder

---

*Missing data are divided into unknown values (that are coded as multiple of 9, e.g., 9, 99, etc., depending upon number of fields used for the variable), and values that are in principle irrelevant to the incident (e.g., if no demands for ransom were made the amount and type of ransom demanded is irrelevant), which are coded with an 8 at the end of the string of 9's. This allows real 9 values to occur for ratio data.

13 sabotage--not involving bombing

14 exotic pollution, including CBW

15 nuclear-related

16 extortionate threat with no subsequent terrorist action

17 other actions

18 hoax

4   TARGET SELECTION

1 indiscriminate selection of targets

2 selective attack on specific targets of symbolic value

5   WARNING--Did group send a warning of attack?

1 yes

2 no

6   LOCATION OF ACTION--NATION

3-digit code for each nation or territory, modified from that developed by Bruce M. Russett, J. David Singer, and Melvin Small, "National Political Units in the Twentieth Century: A Standardized List" 62, 3 <u>American Political Science Review</u> (Sept., 196<u>8</u>), pp. 935-950.

7   LOCATION OF ACTION--ENVIRON

1 urban

2 rural

3 in transit in air or water

8   LOCATION OF ACTION--SCENE OF THE CRIME

1 home of victim; base or installation

2 office

3 motor vehicle, train, aircraft, boat, embarkation area

4 street

5 other

9   GROUP INITIATING ACTION

A 4-digit code unique to each group. Up to 4
groups may be listed. The name of the major
initiator of the action is the first group
listed.

10   ORGANIZATION CLAIMING RESPONSIBILITY FOR ACTION

Same procedure as descriptor 9.

11   ORGANIZATION ACTUALLY RESPONSIBLE FOR ACTION

Same procedure as descriptor 9, which lists
group who was popularly believed responsible,
whereas descriptor 11 notes group who was
responsible according to the most reliable
sources available.

12   TERRORIST GROUPS THAT DENIED RESPONSIBILITY

Same procedure as descriptor 9.

13   NUMBER OF TERRORIST GROUPS INVOLVED IN INCIDENT

14   NATIONALITY OR HOME COUNTRY OF TERRORISTS
DIRECTLY INVOLVED

Up to 4 nationalities may be included.

15   NUMBER OF NATIONALITIES OF TERRORISTS INVOLVED

16   FEDAYEEN Was terrorist group considered
fedayeen?

1 yes

2 no

17   NUMBER OF INDIVIDUAL TERRORISTS INVOLVED IN
INCIDENT

18   NUMBER OF MALE TERRORISTS INVOLVED IN INCIDENT

19   NUMBER OF FEMALE TERRORISTS INVOLVED IN INCIDENT

20   LEADER   Did group have an obvious leader?

         1 yes

         2 no

21   AGE OF GROUP MEMBERS

         2 digits, mean age of group members

22   AGE RANGE OF GROUP MEMBERS

         Difference between ages of oldest and youngest group members

23   EDUCATION OF GROUP MEMBERS (MODE)

         1 illiterate

         2 grade school

         3 high school

         4 some college

         5 college graduate

         6 higher degree

24   HOME COUNTRY OF VICTIMS NOT CITIZENS OF HOST COUNTRY

         Same 3-digit coding as descriptor 6. Up to 4 possible nationalities may be included.

25   NUMBER OF NATIONALITIES OF VICTIMS

26   NUMBER OF HOSTAGES

27   TYPE OF US VICTIM

         1 diplomatic

         2 military

3 other US government

4 commercial, business

5 other nonofficial, e.g., tourist, missionary, student

6 no US involvement as victims

28   HIGHEST RANK OF ANY HOSTAGE

1 Ambassador or chief of mission

2 high-ranking military

3 corporation head

4 low-level diplomat

5 low-ranking military

6 citizen

29   TYPE OF TARGET--IMMEDIATE VICTIMS

1 host government officials

2 foreign diplomats or official nonmilitary

3 host government military

4 foreign military

5 corporation officials

6 prominent opinion leaders

7 private parties, e.g., tourists, mission-aries, students

30   TARGET TYPE

1 people

2 installations, property

3 both

31   NUMBER OF GOVERNMENTS UPON WHOM DEMANDS WERE MADE

32 NUMBER OF SEPARATE ENTITIES UPON WHOM DEMANDS WERE MADE

In addition to governments, include corporations, private individuals, international organizations.

33 IDENTITY OF GOVERNMENTS UPON WHOM DEMANDS WERE MADE

Same 3-digit coding as descriptor 9. Up to 4 governments.

34 IDENTITY OF ENTITIES UPON WHOM DEMANDS WERE MADE

A unique 4-digit number is assigned to nongovernmental entities. Up to 4 entities can be listed.

35 WERE DEMANDS MADE UPON THE HOST GOVERNMENT?

1 yes

2 no

36 ATTRIBUTED PURPOSES OF INCIDENT

1 wringing of specific concessions, e.g., ransom, prisoner release, publication of message

2 causing widespread disorder, demoralizing society, breaking down the existing social order

3 deliberately provoking repression, reprisals and counterterrorism, which may ultimately lead to the collapse of an unpopular government

4 enforce obedience and cooperative behavior

5 punishment of an individual or symbol judged "guilty"

37 WERE DEMANDS FOR MONETARY RANSOM MADE?

1 yes

2 no

38   WERE DEMANDS FOR ARMAMENTS MADE?

1 yes

2 no

39   WAS THE RELEASE OF MEMBERS OF OWN GROUP IMPRISONED DEMANDED?

1 yes

2 no

40   WAS THE RELEASE OF PRISONERS OF OTHER GROUPS DEMANDED?

1 yes

2 no

41   WERE DEMANDS FOR INDEPENDENCE OR SELF-RULE OR TERRITORY IDENTIFIED BY THE GROUP MADE?

1 yes

2 no

42   WERE DEMANDS FOR SPECIFIC POLITICAL CHANGES MADE?

1 yes

2 no

43   WERE DEMANDS FOR AMNESTY, SAFE PASSAGE, OR SAFE HAVEN MADE?

1 yes

2 no

44   WERE DEMANDS TO PUBLISH OR BROADCAST A STATEMENT MADE?

1 yes

2 no

45   WERE DEMANDS TO CHANGE SENTENCES OR PRISONERS MADE?

1 yes

2 no

46   WERE OTHER DEMANDS MADE?

These demands may include the release of all Arab women detained in Israel, an audience with a governmental leader, allowing a relative to leave the country, the closing of transit facilities.

1 yes

2 no

47   WERE TERRORISTS ABLE TO MAKE DEMANDS KNOWN?

1 no

2 no, but authorities were able to determine demands a posteriori

3 yes

4 no, but were logistically capable of making demands

48   WERE ANY DEMANDS MADE?

1 no

2 yes

49   TERRORIST NEGOTIATION BEHAVIOR

1 terrorists lessened demands during negotiations

2 terrorists increased demands during negotiations

3 terrorists did not change demands

4 terrorists substituted demands during negotiations, i.e., it is impossible to state whether the change was an increase or decrease

5 up-the-ante doublecross, i.e., more demands were made after the other side fulfilled their part of the bargain

6 other side agreed to comply, terrorists broke contact

7 no contact for negotiations was ever established

50 TYPE OF TARGET UPON WHOM DEMANDS WERE MADE

1 host government

2 victim's government

3 other foreign government

4 corporate officials

5 international organizations

6 individuals

7 other non-state actors

8 other

9 combination of targets

51 TYPE OF NEGOTIATOR FOR TARGETS

1 police

2 high-ranking host government official

3 lower-level host government official

4 high-ranking victim government official

5 lower-level victim government official

6 high-ranking foreign government official

7 lower-level foreign government official

8 corporate official

9 private parties, family

10 prominent opinion leaders

11 other

52   RESPONSE OF TARGET

1 capitulation

2 stalling, with compromise on demands

3 Bangkok solution, i.e., terrorists drop all demands in return for safe passage out of country

4 no compromise, no shoot-out with terrorists

5 shoot-out with terrorists, or attempt to arrest terrorists, or nationwide search for terrorists with no compromise by target regarding demands

53   OBJECTIVE OF PRESSURE BY VICTIM'S GOVERNMENT TO HOST COUNTRY

1 become firmer in negotiations, do not capitulate

2 stall for time, and be willing to compromise

3 capitulate

4 no pressure was exerted

54   NUMBER WOUNDED--DOMESTIC NONCOMBATANT VICTIMS

55   NUMBER WOUNDED--FOREIGN COUNTRY NONCOMBATANT VICTIMS

56   NUMBER WOUNDED--POLICE OR MILITARY COMBATANTS

57   NUMBER WOUNDED--TERRORISTS

58   NUMBER KILLED--DOMESTIC NONCOMBATANT VICTIMS

59   NUMBER KILLED--FOREIGN COUNTRY NONCOMBATANT VICTIMS

60   NUMBER KILLED--POLICE OR MILITARY COMBATANTS

61   NUMBER KILLED--TERRORISTS

62   DOLLAR VALUE OF OTHER LOSSES

63   NUMBER OF PRISONERS RELEASED

64   NUMBER OF PRISONERS WHOSE RELEASE WAS DE-
        MANDED

65   AMOUNT OF RANSOM PAID in thousands, 6 digits

66   AMOUNT OF RANSOM DEMANDED in thousands, 6
        digits

67   TYPE OF RANSOM DEMANDED

        1 Robin Hood-ransom does not go directly to
          terrorists, but is paid to a group selected
          by the initiators of the action as worthy
          of financing, e.g., poor, children, workers'
          groups

        2 organizational coffers--ransom is paid to
          group

        3 both Robin Hood and organizational coffers

        4 no ransom was demanded

68   AMOUNT OF ROBIN HOOD RANSOM DEMANDED in
        thousands, 6 digits

69   AMOUNT OF ROBIN HOOD RANSOM PAID in thousands,
        6 digits

70   AMOUNT OF ORGANIZATIONAL COFFERS RANSOM DE-
        MANDED

71   AMOUNT OF ORGANIZATIONAL COFFERS RANSOM PAID

72   SOURCE OF RANSOM PAYMENT

        1 government

        2 corporation

        3 family

        4 other, e.g., public collection, other
          private sources

5 no ransom paid

73   FATE OF VICTIMS

    1 no damage nor casualties, hostages released, no capitulation by targets

    2 no damage nor casualties, hostages released, capitulation or compromise by targets

    3 victims killed, no capitulation by targets

    4 victims killed, capitulation or compromise by targets

    5 damaged material, no capitulation by targets

    6 damaged material, capitulation or compromise by targets

    7 victim killed when attempting escape, had been captured

    8 victim successfully escaped, had been captured

    9 victim killed attempting to avoid capture

    10 victim successfully avoided capture

    11 hostages killed in shootout

    12 hostages killed, no provocation, during negotiations

    13 hostages killed during negotiations, terrorist-imposed deadline had expired

    14 damaged material, hostages released, no capitulation

74   NUMBER OF NATIONS PUBLICLY DENYING THAT SAFE HAVEN WOULD BE GRANTED IF REQUEST WERE MADE

75   NUMBER OF NATIONS DENYING SAFE HAVEN AFTER REQUEST WAS MADE

76   IDENTITY OF NATIONS SPONTANEOUSLY DENYING SAFE HAVEN

Same 3-digit nation codes as used in descriptor 9. Up to 4 nations may be included.

77   IDENTITY OF NATIONS DENYING SAFE HAVEN REQUEST

Same procedure as used in descriptor 76.

78   NUMBER OF NATIONS SPONTANEOUSLY GRANTING SAFE HAVEN

79   NUMBER OF NATIONS GRANTING SAFE HAVEN UPON REQUEST

80   IDENTITY OF NATIONS SPONTANEOUSLY GRANTING SAFE HAVEN

Same procedure as used in descriptor 76.

81   IDENTITY OF NATIONS GRANTING SAFE HAVEN UPON REQUEST

Same procedure as used in descriptor 76.

82   ULTIMATE DESTINATION OF GROUP e.g., if sky-jackers, where did they disembark and accept sanctuary?

83   GROUP VIEWS TOWARD OWN DEATH   attributed via observation of group behavior during event

1 suicidal

2 willing to die, prefer not to

3 elaborate getaway plans & execution of plans

4 dropping of demands for safe passage from scene

84   NUMBER OF TERRORISTS DEAD AT SCENE IN SHOOT-OUT

85   NUMBER OF TERRORISTS WHO KILLED THEMSELVES AT THE SCENE

86   NUMBER OF TERRORISTS WHO DIED VIA THE DEATH PENALTY

87   NUMBER OF TERRORISTS WHO RECEIVED A JAIL TERM
      OF 5 OR MORE YEARS

88   NUMBER OF TERRORISTS WHO RECEIVED A LONG JAIL
      TERM AND WHOSE RELEASE WAS DEMANDED IN A SUB-
      SEQUENT INCIDENT

89   NUMBER OF TERRORISTS RECEIVING A LONG JAIL
      TERM WHO WERE FREED DUE TO DEMANDS IN SUBSE-
      QUENT INCIDENT

90   NUMBER OF TERRORISTS WHO RECEIVED A JAIL TERM
      OF LESS THAN 5 YEARS

91   NUMBER OF TERRORISTS WHO RECEIVED A SHORT JAIL
      TERM AND WHOSE RELEASE WAS DEMANDED IN A SUB-
      SEQUENT INCIDENT

92   NUMBER OF TERRORISTS RECEIVING A SHORT JAIL
      TERM WHO WERE FREED DUE TO DEMANDS IN SUBSE-
      QUENT INCIDENT

93   NUMBER OF TERRORISTS FREED BY COURT VERDICT

94   NUMBER OF TERRORISTS WHO ESCAPED CAPTORS EN
      ROUTE TO PRISON OR IN PRISON

95   NUMBER OF TERRORISTS WHO WERE GRANTED SAFE
      HAVEN IN A BANGKOK SOLUTION

96   NUMBER OF TERRORISTS WHO WERE ARRESTED BUT
      NOT BROUGHT TO TRIAL e.g., freedom obtained
      by other than court verdict or escape, or who
      "surrendered" to a friendly government

97   WAS REQUEST FOR EXTRADITION MADE?

      1 yes

      2 no

98   IDENTITY OF NATION REQUESTING EXTRADITION

      Same 3-digit nation code as used in descript-
      or 9.

99   WAS EXTRADITION REQUEST GRANTED?

      1 yes

2 no

3 extradition request was not made

100   IDENTITY OF NATION RECEIVING EXTRADITION RE-QUEST

101   DATE OF ENDING OF INCIDENT month day year

102   LENGTH IN DAYS OF INCIDENT

103   WERE US CITIZENS VICTIMS OF THE ATTACK?

1 yes

2 no

104   WERE US SHIPS OR AIRCRAFT INVOLVED?

1 yes

2 no

105   WERE US OFFICIAL INSTALLATIONS INVOLVED?

1 yes

2 no

106   WERE US CORPORATIONS INVOLVED

1 yes

2 no

107   WAS THE US GOVERNMENT A TARGET OF DEMANDS?

1 yes

2 no

Notes

1. A listing of works taking such approaches can be found in Vita Bite, "International Terrorism," Issue Brief Number IB74042 (Washington, D.C.: Library of Congress, CRS, October 31, 1975); Roger Cosyns-Verhaegen, *Present-Day Terrorism: Bibliographical Selection* (Wavre, Belgium: Centre D'Information et de Documentation de la. L.I.L., 1973); Edward Hyams, *Terrorists and Terrorism* (London: J. M. Dent, 1975); and Edward F. Mickolus, *Annotated Bibliography on Transnational and International Terrorism* PR 76 10073U (Washington, D.C.: Central Intelligence Agency, December 1976).

2. Brian Michael Jenkins and Janera Johnson, "International Terrorism: A Chronology, 1968-1974," R-1597-DOS/ARPA (Santa Monica: The RAND Corporation, March 1975).

3. For definitions of these types of incidents, see Edward F. Mickolus, "Trends in Transnational Terrorism," *Terrorism in the Contemporary World*, ed. Marius Livingstone (Westport, Conn.: Greenwood Press, 1978); and Edward F. Mickolus, "Transnational Terrorism," *The Politics of Terror: A Reader in Theory and Practice*, ed. Michael Stohl (New York: Marcel Dekker, 1978).

4. ITERATE is now available through the Inter-University Consortium for Political and Social Research, P.O. Box 1248, Ann Arbor, Michigan 48106, as a Class II data set. In their 1976 catalog, ICPSR lists the data set's order number as ICPSR 7486.

5. Only incidents of transnational terrorism, as defined, are included. Events related to the Vietnam conflict are not included, nor are the numerous cross-border raids between Arabs and Israelis against military targets. Plots to engage in actions classified as terrorist, but which were discovered before the carrying out of the operation, are not included, nor are threats to engage in such actions (although such events may be included in future versions of ITERATE). Although the present computerized version of ITERATE includes only the RAND chronology, statistics for the tables presented herein were hand-calculated from the RAND chronology plus forty other unclassified data sources. A list of these sources is available on request.

6. Attempted skyjackings which were thwarted on the ground are not counted. To qualify for inclusion in the present study, such attacks must have the attributes of our definition of transnational terrorism. Incidents which did not involve a crossing of a border (such as events

involving the payment of ransom and parachuting of the hijacker from the plane within the territorial confines of the nation of embarkation), domestic attempts to hijack a plane to another county which involve no injuries in the resolution of the incident, and incidents which involved only one nationality of passengers, crew, perpetrator, destination, and embarkation point of the flight are thus not included. Although sky-jackings and nonair takeovers can become barricade-and-hostage situations, these incidents are not treated as barricade-and-hostage if they occurred in transit. Hence, the multiple skyjackings of the Popular Front for the Liberation of Palestine in September 1970 are treated as skyjackings, even though negotiations were conducted on the ground.

7. A score of definitions have been offered for the term "assassination." Rather than attempt to distinguish between the political murder of a low-level official and a high-level official (if such an arbitrary cutoff point could be established with any meaning), determine the motivations of the killer, etc., and become a part of a definitional debate as unproductive as that on "terrorism," a general category of political murder and assassination is employed. To qualify for inclusion, such acts must satisfy the conditions of the definition of international terrorism.

8. The location of an incident is considered to be the place in which the incident began. Its date is that date in which it became known to individuals other than the terrorists that a terrorist incident was taking place. In the case of skyjacking, the location is the nation in which the plane had last touched ground before the hijackers made their presence as hijackers known. In cases in which the embarkation point is not known, the location is considered to be that nation in which the plane landed and the negotiations took place. If neither of the above apply, the nation of registry is used.

The location of an incident need not be a nation-state. Protectorates, colonies, and mandated territories may also experience terrorism, and the responsible government considers them to be different types of security and administrative environments. Hence, such areas as Puerto Rico and Gibraltar are included as locations, despite the legal citizenship of their residents.

9. For a more complete cataloging of the arguments involved, see Edward F. Mickolus, "Negotiating for Hostages: A Policy Dilemma" *Orbis* 19, no. 4 (Winter 1976): 1309-1325.

10. See Ernest Evans, "American Policy Response to International

Terrorism,'' paper presented to the Conference on Terrorism in the Contemporary World, held at Glassboro State College, April 26-28, 1976. Note also Evans' dissertation for the MIT Department of Political Science.

11. David L. Milbank, *Research Study: International and Transnational Terrorism; Diagnosis and Prognosis* PR 76 10030 (Washington, D.C.: Central Intelligence Agency, April 1976).

8

Multidimensional Scaling of UN Voting Behavior

Robin S. Kent and Winston P. Wiley

During 1974 U.S. policymakers became increasingly concerned with the successful use of bloc voting practices in the UN General Assembly by the members of the Third World, often in opposition to U.S. voting positions. One response to this trend was intensification of the practice of ranking states according to how often they "supported" the United States. The obvious limitations of this approach—it is too simple to accommodate the variety of issues voted on, and it cannot distinguish degrees of opposition or support—made it both intellectually and practically unsatisfactory. This approach also failed to answer what were becoming increasingly important corollary questions: (1) the extent to which the voting position of the Third World countries was monolithic, and (2) the existence of subgroupings which could be identified on the basis of regional or substantive differences.[1]

One of the responses to the perception of increased Third World cohesion in the UN General Assembly was the development by CIA of a computerized data base of UN voting records.[2] This was followed by research by the authors, in

This is a slightly edited version of a paper presented at the Eighteenth Annual Convention of the International Studies Association in St. Louis, March 1977.

TABLE 1

LEVEL OF AGREEMENT BETWEEN THE UNITED STATES
AND THE UNITED KINGDOM, 1970 - 1975

1970	89.55%
1971	80.95%
1972	89.55%
1973	90.00%
1974	85.53%
1975	87.24%

conjunction with a private contractor, on methods to measure cohesion in voting patterns among a group of countries and the means to identify clusters of countries with similar voting patterns.[3] Multidimensional scaling was selected as having some potential for this purpose because of its ability to handle relatively large numbers of countries and issues simultaneously, and because the graphic output is readily understandable to the nonmethodologically trained policy official.[4]

It is important to note at this point that the interest in these voting patterns was not based on how accurately the votes represented the Third World's positions in the larger political arena, but on the votes themselves. The well-known limitations that exist in studying UN voting patterns as a surrogate for what is going on in the broader international environment, therefore, did not apply or limit the range of analytical responses to the question.

Most quantitative techniques that had been applied previously to UN voting by intelligence and policy analysts involved the calculation of the level of agreement between two nations.[5] One such calculation produces indices of agreement such as those shown in Table 1.

Other approaches had dealt with the cohesion exhibited

TABLE 2

COHESION OF NONALIGNED STEERING GROUP
ON THREE SELECTED RESOLUTIONS, 1975

Resolution	Yes	Abstain	No	Cohesion Index
3390	2	5	10	52.94%
3395	17	0	0	100.00%
3458	6	7	6	0.00%

by a group of nations on a specific resolution or set of resolutions. Various indices of cohesion have been developed which describe the amount of internal agreement that is manifested by the group. An example is shown in Table 2.

Both of these examples rely on a single number that describes the level of agreement or the amount of cohesion. Indices of this kind cannot provide answers to such questions as:

- Which nations in the group vote together most frequently? Which show the least agreement?
- What is the relationship of the group's members to a specific nation of interest such as the U.S.?
- Are there identifiable subgroups? Do voting relationships change across different sets of issues?

Multidimensional scaling is one technique for getting answers to these questions.[6] In essence, this approach permits the analyst to construct a visual model of the political relationship being studied. The relationship may be represented in one, two, three, or more dimensions. In this case, the relationship being studied is the voting behavior of a group of UN members. Taken as a whole, these votes represent a set of attitudes expressed by the members of the group toward the issues on which they voted. The advantage of the technique is that the model can be easily understood by readers who may know or care very little about the intricacies of quantitative techniques. Thus, the analyst can utilize the model itself to quickly convey analytical judgments to the policymaker.

In this study, we examined first the voting positions of a "representative" set of thirty-six nations during the 1975 General Assembly.[7] The nations were selected by an analyst familiar with the issues and general voting patterns during the 1975 session. The criterion for selection was simply to create a group that included the major powers and several representative nations from each geographic region. The composition of the group is shown in Table 3.

Multidimensional scaling requires some measurement of the similarity between every pair of objects (in this case, UN members) making up the group. The measurements utilized here are correlation coefficients. Thus, two nations which show a high positive coefficient have very similar voting characteristics. Conversely, a pair of nations having a strong negative coefficient tend to vote against each other on most issues.

Being a nonmetric technique, multidimensional scaling does not force the analyst to make the strong assumptions required by factor analysis. It requires only that the ranking of the correlation coefficients be valid; they need not be considered a precise measurement of similarity.[8]

These measurements are utilized to produce a plot or model of the set of voting attitudes. Nations which have similar voting patterns are positioned close to each other on the plot; nations which differ are located farther apart. A measure of the "goodness" of the plot—the "stress" value— serves as the basic criterion for determining whether a multidimensional configuration is satisfactory.[9]

As a first step, a multidimensional scaling analysis was

TABLE 3

MEMBERS OF REPRESENTATIVE GROUP OF NATIONS

US and Western Europe:
- US
- Austria
- France
- Greece
- Netherlands
- Spain
- Turkey
- United Kingdom

Eastern Europe:
- Albania
- Yugoslavia
- USSR

Latin America:
- Bahamas
- Brazil
- Colombia
- Cuba
- Guatemala
- Mexico
- Uruguay

Africa:
- Central Africa
- Ivory Coast
- Kenya
- Mauritania
- Nigeria
- Tanzania

Middle East:
- Israel
- Jordan
- Libya
- Morocco
- Saudi Arabia
- Yemen

Asia:
- Burma
- China
- India
- Japan
- Mongolia
- Singapore

Figure 1

VOTING OF REPRESENTATIVE NATIONS ON ALL ISSUES, 1975

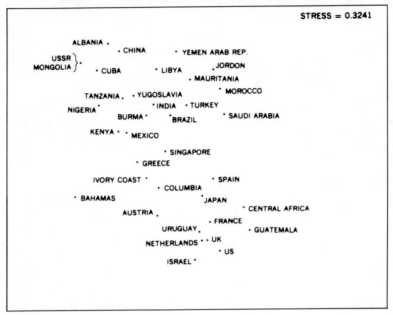

Figure 1 reflects the general voting environment of the 1975 General Assembly: the antagonism between the Third World and communist nations, on the one hand, and a dwindling group of Western allies, on the other. Most Latin

made of the group's behavior of all ninety-eight recorded votes during the plenary sessions of the 1975 General Assembly. The two-dimensional result is shown in Figure 1. The stress value (0.3241) for this solution is only fair. The three-dimensional solution is somewhat better (0.2581) but cannot be represented here. Given the broad range of issues included in these ninety-eight votes, such a result should be expected.

American and European states had closer affinity for the U.S. voting positions than for the opposite extreme. Nevertheless, three of those nations—Turkey, Brazil, and Mexico—voted fairly consistently with the Third World position. The Middle Eastern nations demonstrated the greatest solidarity of any noncommunist group. The African nations showed no clear pattern. The Central African Republic, for example, is seen to be more closely associated with the Latin American and Western European states than with the more radical African nations such as Tanzania or Mauritania.

Analysts and policy officials were also concerned with determining whether the members of the UN (represented here by the selected group of nations) voted in the same way across a broad range of issues, or whether different patterns emerged when issue areas changed. Figures 2 and 3 show the representative nations' voting patterns on Middle Eastern issues and African issues.[10] It should be said that using only one issue area (which also can be identified through factor analysis of UN voting) does not distort multidimensional scaling methodology from our perspective, because our goal was to identify general affinity groups, not to array countries along clearly identifiable issue dimensions.

On Middle Eastern issues (most of these votes dealt with the Zionism-as-racism question), affinity groups are much more easily identified than when all ninety-eight plenary issues are considered. Note in Figure 2 that Tanzania, Cuba, India, Jordan, Yugoslavia, the USSR, Mongolia, and Saudi Arabia are located on the same point, showing near complete agreement on this set of votes. Yemen, Mauritania, Morocco, Turkey, Brazil and Libya are located close enough that they too can be considered to be virtually identical to the first group. Some support for the U.S.-backed Israeli position is also clearly identifiable, but the decreasing degree of support by individual nations ranging from the United States to

Figure 2

VOTING OF REPRESENTATIVE NATIONS ON MIDEAST ISSUES, 1975

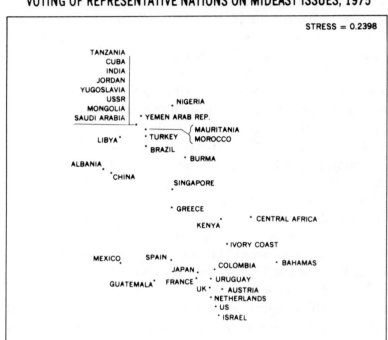

Colombia is also clear. The ambivalence of countries such as Singapore, Greece, Kenya and the Central African Republic is also evident from their location midway between the two main clusters.

Figure 3 shows the distribution of the representative nations on African issues, primarily dealing with condemnation of the regimes of South Africa and Rhodesia and some votes critical of the U.S. imports of chrome from those nations. It can be seen that some of the tight groupings identified on

Figure 3

VOTING OF REPRESENTATIVE NATIONS ON AFRICAN ISSUES, 1975

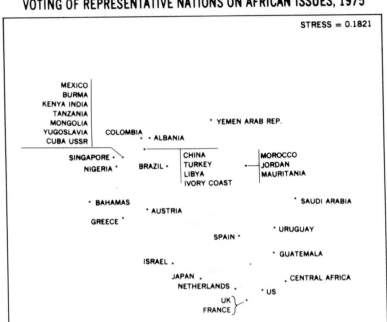

Middle Eastern issues have disappeared, and some new alliances have become apparent. Overall, the general distribution showed no major shifts from Figure 2 with two exceptions. Colombia, whose position is relatively close to the U.S. position in Figure 1 (all issues) and Figure 2 (Middle Eastern issues), finds itself at the far end of the spectrum on African issues. A review of the sixteen votes indicates that Colombia in fact opposed the United States on almost all of the African votes. Mexico, which occupied a middle position in Figure 1 (all issues) and a position near the United States in Figure 2

Figure 4

VOTING OF LATIN AMERICAN NATIONS ON AFRICAN ISSUES, 1975

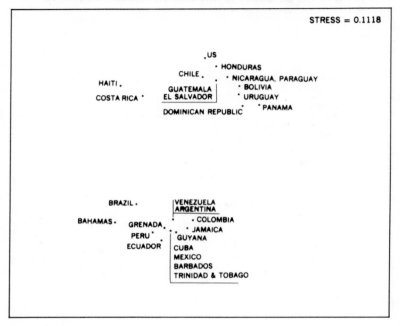

(Middle Eastern issues), also voted against the United States on the African issues. The reasons for the apparent shift in their voting patterns cannot, of course, be explained on the basis of this kind of analysis, but the procedure did highlight important shifts in voting behavior of which most analysts were unaware.

Figure 4 shows the distribution of all South American countries on the sixteen African resolutions. Mexico's and Colombia's radical positions are again seen. More importantly, however, it should be noted that they have extensive company, including all the major Latin American states.

Figure 5 shows the distribution of the representative

Figure 5

VOTING OF REPRESENTATIVE NATIONS
ON MIDEAST & AFRICAN ISSUES, 1975

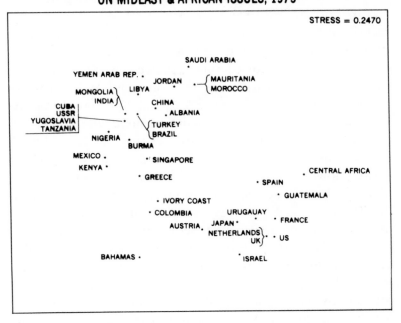

nations when the sixteen African and twenty-eight Middle Eastern issues are combined. As might be expected, the positions of the nations show no significant change from Figures 2 and 3, with the exception of Colombia and Mexico. Two major groups can be identified. In the upper part of the chart, we find the leaders of the Third World, ranging from such radicals as Tanzania in the lower left to the conservative Saudi Arabian position in the upper right. The group on the bottom, including the United States, is composed of generally more conservative states, but differences between Bahamas and Central African Republic appear to mirror those between

Tanzania and Saudi Arabia. Mexico, Singapore, and Greece, as they did in Figure 1, demonstrate an ambivalence on these issues.

In addition to its utility for identifying the differences in a group's voting behavior across different sets of issues, multidimensional scaling enables the policymaker to understand how different groups of nations behave on a selected set of resolutions. Figure 5, discussed above, showed the distribution of the representative nations on the forty-four Middle Eastern and African resolutions. Figures 6, 7, and 8 portray the behavior of three selected regional groups on these same votes.

At first glance, Figure 6 indicates that the Latin American nations form two distinct voting subgroups. The lower cluster, however, is far less cohesive than the group associated with the United States. For example, the distance between the Bahamas and Brazil is greater than the distance between the Bahamas and the United States. It seems likely, therefore, that two categories exist within the lower cluster. The first, a "hard-core" group, consists of Cuba, Guyana, Grenada, Mexico, Peru, Jamaica, and Trinidad and Tobago. This group consistently voted the Third World position on both the African and Middle Eastern issues. The remaining nations located below the horizontal axis voted with the Third World more often than not, but were less consistent. Colombia, which voted very differently on Middle Eastern and African issues, is the best example of this behavior pattern (see Figures 2 and 3).

The African states, in Figure 7, demonstrate far less cohesion. Nevertheless, three general groups can be identified. The most congenial group from the U.S. point of view included the Central African Republic, Gabon, Togo, Zaire, Liberia, Ivory Coast Malawi, and Swaziland. Their relative proximity to the United States is based primarily on their abstention on many of the Zionism-as-racism issues; there

Figure 6

VOTING OF LATIN AMERICAN NATIONS
ON MIDEAST & AFRICAN ISSUES, 1975

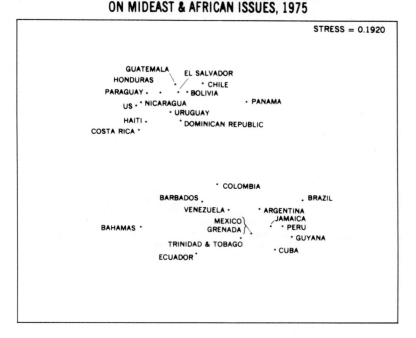

was virtual unanimity on most of the southern African questions. It should be noted that this group is quite disparate. For example, the distance between Malawi and Central Africa is about equal to the distance bewteen Malawi and Burundi, the nation most antagonistic to the United States on these issues.

The second group, including Gambia, Sao Tome, Cape Verde, Mauritius, Mauritania, Sudan, Senegal, Rwanda, and Cameroon, shows a high degree of common interest, significant differences from the United States, and a common distance from the third group which includes all of the other African states. This graph demonstrates how this technique

Figure 7

VOTING OF AFRICAN NATIONS ON MIDEAST & AFRICAN ISSUES, 1975

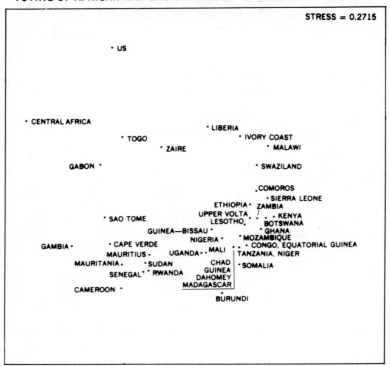

can be used to stimulate further research with other methods. In this case analysts might decide to test the hypothesis that a high degree of economic dependence on Western countries led to moderation on some of the blatantly political aspects of the Zionism-as-racism resolutions.

Figure 8 shows that the members of the Organization for Economic Cooperation and Development (OECD) are generally very similar in their voting behavior. The main cluster shows a span from the more liberal Nordic regimes towards

Figure 8

VOTING OF OECD NATIONS ON MIDEAST & AFRICAN ISSUES, 1975

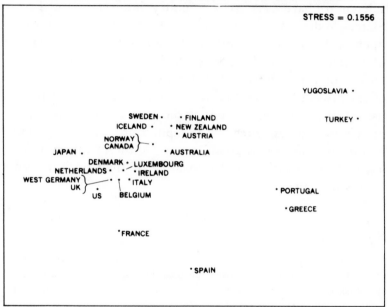

the United States, while the maverick roles of France, Spain, Yugoslavia (an associate member of the OECD), Turkey, Portugal, and Greece are highlighted. Figures 1 through 5 showed the latter two countries more closely identified with the positions of the Third World.

In conclusion, it can be said that multidimensional scaling has been useful in meeting the limited goals that were set from the start. Most of the findings confirmed the assumptions of regional specialists about the behavior of the various UN members, although some counter-intuitive results (e.g., Columbia and Mexico on African issues) did stimulate further study. Publication of preliminary findings and a description

of the method also led to a series of special studies on how
certain countries voted across a range of issues that were considered to have been of key policy interest to the United
States. Multidimensional scaling also provided the basis for
opening discussions among analysts about the voting behavior
of certain states in the UN by providing a relatively objective
"map" of voting behavior. The most rewarding consequence
of the project has been the stimulation of requests for further
use of this method. Potential subjects for analysis include
nonvoting bodies, such as the politburo of a communist
nation, whenever it is possible to scale the members according to the similarity or dissimilarity of their positions on a
variety of issues.

Notes

1. There have been numerous academic studies of voting behavior
in the United Nations. See, for example, Hayward R. Alker and Bruce
M. Russett, *World Politics in the General Assembly* (1965); Arend
Lijphart, "The Analysis of Bloc Voting in the General assembly: A
Critique and a Proposal," *American Political Science Review* 57, no. 4
(December 1963); Leroy N. Rieselbach, "Quantitative Techniques for
Studying Voting Behavior in the UN General Assembly," *International
Organization* 14, no. 2 (Spring 1960); Bruce M. Russett, "Discovering
Voting Groups in the United Nations," *American Political Science
Review* 60, no. 2 (June 1966); and Hanna Newcombe et al., "United
Nations Voting Patterns," *International Organization* 24, no. 1 (Winter
1970).

2. The data base developed by CIA was based upon a system built
by the U.S. Naval Academy Political Science Department and the
Office of Management Systems in the U.S. Department of State.

3. See Richard Van Atta and Leo Hazelwood, "Cohesion in the
Group of 77" (Arlington, Va.: CACI, Inc., January 1976) and "Mea-
sures of Voting Cohesion and Agreement for Analyzing the United
Nations" (Arlington, Va.: CACI, Inc., March 1976).

4. The general term, multidimensional scaling, embraces a wide
range of data analysis techniques. It refers here, however, to the set of

techniques developed by Roger N. Shepard and J. B. Kruskal at Bell Laboratories. See Roger N. Shepard, A. Kimball Romney, and Sara Beth Nerlove, eds., *Multidimensional Scaling,* 2 vols. (New York: Seminar Press, 1972).

5. There are several methods for measuring the amount of agreement between two nations. The most commonly used is:

$$IVC = \frac{a + \frac{1}{2}(g)}{t}$$

where IVC = Index of Voting Cohesion

   a = Number of resolutions on which both nations voted the same

   g = Number of resolutions on which one nation abstained and the other voted yes or no

   t = Total number of resolutions

6. Factor analysis is another approach that has been utilized to answer questions of this nature. See, for example, Bruce M. Russett, *op. cit.* The results generated by factor analysis, however, are often too complex for easy presentation to the policymaker.

7. The size of the group was limited to a maximum of forty-two by the limitations of the multidimensional scaling computer program.

8. See J. B. Kruskal, "Non-metric Multidimensional Scaling: A Numerical Method," *Psychometrika* 29 (June 1964): 115-130.

9. The guideline developed by Kruskal for interpreting stress is as follows:

Excellent	0.000-0.100
Good	0.101-0.200
Fair	0.201-0.400
Poor	0.401-1.000

10. Each recorded vote in the computerized file is coded according to its general subject matter and regional focus. Thus, the user is able to retrieve only those votes coded as "Middle Eastern," "African" or any combination desired. During the 1975 General Assembly there were twenty-eight recorded votes coded as dealing with the Middle Eastern area while sixteen were coded as relating to the African region.